CREATIVE
BOOT CAMP

GENERATE IDEAS IN GREATER QUANTITY & QUALITY IN 30 DAYS

STEFAN MUMAW

New Riders

VOICES THAT MATTER™

Creative Boot Camp: Generate Ideas in Greater Quantity & Quality in 30 Days
Stefan Mumaw

New Riders
www.newriders.com

To report errors, please send a note to: errata@peachpit.com

New Riders is an imprint of Peachpit, a division of Pearson Education.

Copyright © 2013 by Stefan Mumaw

Acquisitions Editor: Nikki McDonald
Project Editor: Rebecca Gulick
Development and Copy Editor: Anne Marie Walker
Production Coordinator: Rebecca Chapman-Winter
Interior and Cover Designer and Compositor: Stefan Mumaw
Proofreader: Patricia J. Pane
Indexer: Valerie Haynes Perry
Toy Army Men Photography: Jon Hardesty

ISBN-13: 978-0-321-88464-0
ISBN-10: 0-321-88464-7

9 8 7 6 5 4 3 2 1
Printed and bound in the United States of America

In Greek mythology, muses were the goddesses of inspiration. Homer wrote of nine muses that spanned literature, science, and the arts. He counted only nine because he had never met my daughter, Caitlyn.

This book is dedicated to The Goose, the tenth muse. She is mine.

ABOUT THE AUTHOR

My name is Stefan Mumaw, and I am the Creative Director and Purveyor of All That Rocks at Callahan Creek, a Kansas City, Missouri-area ad agency. For most of my professional life, I have been fascinated with the creative process. As a designer, I've explored creative solutions for big and small brands alike, from Sony and Pioneer to Royal Canin and Westar Energy. As a writer, I've had the opportunity to research how other talented creatives employ their creative processes and inserted the best of what I discovered into six books on design, creativity, and advertising. As a speaker, I've had the privilege of speaking to groups large and small about how the creative process changes from person to person and group to group. As a workshop leader, I've been honored to show teams of creatives how to find innovation and joy in their processes.

What I've discovered through it all is that despite the fears of virtually every creative on the planet, the next idea always comes. It may not be at the time you prefer or in the format you expect, but it will present itself. One of the greatest joys I have in creative leadership is being there the moment it does.

I wrote Creative Boot Camp to help you realize more of those moments. They are what bring every creative back to the table time and time again. When you generate ideas in greater quantity and quality, those ideas become someone else's inspiration to do the same. If we play our cards right, you and I could play a part in the next world-changing idea. That possibility rocks. I should know, I'm the purveyor.

ACKNOWLEDGMENTS

I would first like to thank my wife, Niqua, for her love and compassion, and for keeping the household running while I sequestered myself in my office to put all of this down on paper. I'd like to thank my daughter, Caitlyn, for understanding her role as novelty maker in my life. I'd like to thank my mom for telling me every day that I would be fantastic. I'd like to thank my friend and Executive Creative Director, Tug McTighe, for a steady stream of inspiration, energy, and movie quotes. I'd like to thank my Acquisitions Editor, Nikki McDonald, for her persistence and understanding despite flaking on lunch multiple times. I'd like to thank my Project Editor, Rebecca Gulick, for the well-oiled machine that kept this book on track. I'd like to thank Anne Marie Walker, the single greatest Development Editor I've ever worked with. I'd like to thank the man that I would consider my creative mentor, Sam Harrison, even if he doesn't know it yet. I'd like to thank my dear creative friends Von Glitschka, Justin Ahrens, David Sherwin, Darcy Hinrichs, Jenn and Ken Visocky O'Grady (and Petals), Chris Elkerton, Wendy Oldfield, Trevor Gerhard, Jim Krause, Crystal Reynolds, Cami Travis-Groves, and Karen Larson for the laughs, the ideas, and the constant encouragement. I'd like to thank Jeremy Gard for his friendship, banter, and code rangerness. But most of all, I'd like to thank my Lord and God for giving me all of them.

CONTENTS

SECTION 2: NUMBKILLER

INTRODUCTION

Boot Camp is a military term that describes basic training for recruits. It's used as an indoctrination into the culture of the corps and helps prepare the necessary skills needed to succeed as a soldier.

Creative Boot Camp takes this same immersive model and applies it to basic creative training. It will be used to indoctrinate you into the culture of ideation and will help prepare the necessary skills you need to succeed as a creative.

And shaved heads are not a requirement unless you want one; then by all means shave your head.

Tell me if any of this sounds familiar.

Four days in the summer of 2004 changed my life. I had graduated from college eight years prior with a degree in Communication Arts and had been practicing graphic design professionally and recreationally. I was captivated by design and still am, but as much as I loved art, on its own the art wasn't enough. I was drawn to the subject of the art, the central focus of the design: the idea. I began to explore other mediums: writing, photography, and coding. Never before had I really explored any of these mediums, but I felt my passion for design beginning to wane. My interest was spreading and expanding into other areas. It wasn't until I embarked on a surprise trip to San Diego that summer that I found out why.

In a last-minute decision, my agency sent me to a design conference in San Diego. I'd never been to this conference or any other design conference for that matter. It was a four-day affair, complete with sessions and workshops, networking opportunities and parties, and conversations in the hallways and across hotel lounges. For those four days, I took 31 pages of notes. I just couldn't stop. Every speaker offered insights and processes different than my own; every random conversation sparked ideas and possibilities. I picked up few usable productivity tips but a wealth of process experiments, philosophical explorations, and energy boosters.

I returned from the conference as fired up as I had ever been professionally. It was like returning from camp as a kid. It was the type of experience where you come back all hopped up to make strange new things with odd new skills, with a confidence that's uniquely tied to being forced into a comfort-zone annihilation.

Unlike camp, however, that feeling didn't slowly fade. And I didn't return to the person I had been. My energy kept building. I designed more, wrote better, and conjured up more and better ideas. Before long I had a list of projects I wanted to undertake, and instead of that list starting strong and petering out, it kept growing.

How was this possible? How did I go to a conference focused on the execution of ideas and return with an increasing desire and ability to generate ideas in greater quantity and quality? I didn't attend any sessions emphasizing ideation *directly*. I received no formal idea training, nor did I learn any new brainstorming techniques while I was there. How could I explain this increase in the caliber of the ideas I was generating?

After some time away from the experience and some reflection, the answer became clear: *immersion*.

For those four days, I was immersed in an idea culture. I was surrounded by people who were in the habit of generating ideas and seeking new ways to do so. They had their own processes, perspectives, and experiences, and they were there to soak up the processes, perspectives, and experiences of others. The value of the conference had little to do with the subject matter presented from the stage and everything to do with the immersion in a creative culture hell-bent on bettering everything about the process. By immersing myself into this culture, even for a relatively short period of time, I was consciously and subconsciously focusing on my craft one conversation at a time. And that's when I realized that what I love isn't design, *it's ideas*.

WHAT IS CREATIVE IMMERSION?

I could never put my finger on what attracted me to the design industry until I attended the conference. It is the idea—not the execution—that drives my design addiction. I was, and still am, obsessed with finding solutions to problems. So much so that I began to research and explore how others—individuals and groups—solve problems. I was hooked on exploring the creative process—my own and others'.

I learned that as much as I feared never generating another good idea, I always did. And the more that I studied and practiced the creative process, the better those ideas became. I was generating more ideas faster, and the quality of those ideas was getting better. The more I immersed myself in the act of ideation, the better I became at it.

That is the purpose of this book: immersion. This book is not an in-depth, scientific look at convergent and divergent thinking or an exploration of how the two halves of the brain work. This book isn't about a magic pill or a revolutionary new creative process. This book is about *creative immersion*. As you'll see throughout the program, creativity isn't some mystical, unknowable force. Creativity is a skill. And as with any skill, you can improve your creativity with practice. Throughout this book, I'll expose you to techniques and processes that encourage you to practice creative thinking. By the end of 30 days, you'll be able to see a noticeable and measurable increase in your creative output.

But don't expect boot camp to be easy. It won't take much time out of your day to immerse yourself in this culture. But the time you spend will not be a cakewalk. It will be fun, of this you can be sure, but it will take dedication and effort. It will require that, like any camp, you abandon your comfort zone. Occasionally, the program will ask you to put aside your pride and your position. It will implore you to be honest and forthright with where you are creatively. It will request that you look beyond your known and mastered fields of interest and execute in mediums you may find foreign.

You won't be very good at the start, but you'll get noticeably better if you follow the program with integrity, passion, and drive. As with many things in life, you will get out of this program what you put into it. If you skate through, take days off, don't engage in certain exercises, and are distracted, indifferent, or unresponsive, you'll find little value here. However, if you dedicate yourself to the program, you'll generate ideas in greater quantity and quality in a short period of time.

WHAT IF I'M NOT A DESIGNER?

This is not solely a designer's book: Writers, photographers, illustrators, coders, marketers, men, women, aliens, cowboys, and woodland animals with opposable thumbs and a penchant for literature will also benefit. Despite the title of "creative" being held hostage by the design community, we are all creative. We all benefit from novel ideas that solve problems. We all want to solve problems quickly and deftly. The exercises and processes in the program are meant to develop the problem-solving mentality needed for any creative endeavor. This book won't teach you to be a better designer or writer or photographer, although it may help. This book will teach you to develop stronger ideas faster. Don't get wrapped up in the quality of the drawing you made or the dangling participle in the story you wrote. Don't bypass an exercise because you don't think you can draw or because you believe you are a terrible photographer. Don't judge the quality of your execution; simply focus on the quality of the idea behind it.

Thomas Edison once said, "We shall have no better conditions in the future if we are satisfied with all those which we have at present." As part of this program, you will be exposed to techniques that will take you beyond your comfort level. When the program encourages you to find a partner and engage in an improv comedy drill or pushes you to find accountability from another, fear not, for Edison's better conditions will be the ultimate reward.

HOW DIFFICULT WILL THIS PROGRAM BE?

I am a big believer in making creative training fun. Finding the unexpected solution is addictive because it is an act of joy. Albert Einstein characterized creativity as "intelligence having fun," and that's what this book strives to achieve. Don't take yourself too seriously as you go through the program. As boot camps go, this one won't ask you to run ten miles before breakfast or crawl in the mud. That is, of course, unless crawling in the mud is your solution to a problem posed in the program; then by all means, feel free.

Fun is the true in-progress measurement to the effectiveness of this program. If you aren't having fun as you're doing these exercises, you're not doing them right. The more fun you have, the easier ideas will come.

Do me a favor: Recall an instance in your life when ideas flowed fast and freely, a specific time when you were throwing out ideas over a conference table, or a bar, or wherever. Maybe you were with a group of people, or maybe you were alone. But something triggered a torrent of ideas. Remember back to that time with as much color and feeling as you can. Can you see it? Is the picture there? Good. Now tell me this: Wasn't it *fun*?

I'm betting it was. The joy that comes with every new idea is what fuels you to be the best designer, writer, or photographer that you can be. Don't lose the joy in this process. It is what makes you creative.

Does any of this sound familiar? In 30 days, it will.

THE SHOPPING CART ROLE MODEL

Let me tell you a story about a shopping cart and what it can teach you about the creative process.

In 1999, CBS Nightline aired a report called "The Deep Dive," which was a segment that explored the product development firm IDEO. In this report, CBS Nightline approached IDEO with a proposition: *We want to give you a problem to solve, set some restrictions, and then film your process as you solve it. The project is to redesign the common shopping cart in five days.*

If you don't know IDEO, the company doesn't rely solely on product design experts in any particular field or industry. IDEO has a creative process its employees believe in strongly, and they apply that process to anything from toy dinosaurs to space shuttles. It fills its idea teams with an eclectic mix of people from inside and outside of its corporate structure, and it has no discernible corporate hierarchy during ideation. Everyone is equal because insight, perspective, and experience can come from anyone. IDEO is responsible for some of the most innovative product designs you may or may not have ever recognized. From Apple's first mouse to the squishy grip on just about every toothbrush manufactured today, IDEO can and has applied its creative process to a myriad of items and found a plethora of useful, beautiful design solutions.

So when CBS Nightline asked IDEO to redesign the common shopping cart, an apparatus that has changed little since its inception in the late 1930s, the company jumped at the opportunity to apply its creative process to "the problem." IDEO calls this process The Deep Dive, which is defined as a total immersion in the problem at hand. The creatives met as a group and then broke into teams to start researching how shopping carts are used, manufactured, and stored. They observed how people used the carts in stores; talked to experts on materials, storage, and mobility; and returned from their first full day on the project to enlighten the other groups of their findings.

SOLVING THE PROBLEMS

Problem solving began the next day. Each group started sketching, posting, building, prototyping, modeling, and discussing. The groups presented possibilities to the other groups, brainstorming and sharing thoughts on other possible solutions. They built makeshift models to test theories, often failing to satisfy the objective at hand. Failure, however, is looked upon favorably at IDEO. One of its mantras is "Fail often to succeed sooner." The failures didn't seem to affect the groups; teams continued to build on the ideas, taking bits and pieces of failures and successes to try something new. Another mantra at IDEO is "One conversation at a time," but this didn't stop teams from sketching and drawing as another team presented its findings or offered opinions. The atmosphere was almost chaotic. But when asked if this was the definition of "organized chaos," CEO David Kelley replied, "Not organized chaos, focused chaos."

As the groups offered idea after idea, a small group of self-appointed "adults," consisting of Kelley, project lead Peter Skillman, and a few others, huddled together to create a plan to ensure that the project stayed on track. "Creativity is a messy process," Kelley explained. "You can't work without time constraints or else it will just keep going." They assigned teams to solve the four primary problems that the groups uncovered: shopping, safety, checkout, and finding what you are looking for. (Notice that the problems they were solving weren't just about the shopping cart; they were also about shopping. The cart was just a tool to solve greater problems.)

The teams began working on solutions, which meant more prototyping, testing, sketching, and discussing. They built models to present the culmination of their best ideas, focusing solely on the problem they were assigned. No one person was given the task of redesigning the entire cart; nor was one person even tasked with solving one of the four primary problems determined during the exploratory phase. The end result would be a team solution in every facet, and this was by design. "Enlightened trial and error succeeds over the planning of the lone genius," Skillman said. You would think that the prototyping failures piling up would have a negative effect on the morale of the group, but the mood was much livelier than expected. This, too, was by design. "Being playful is of huge importance to being innovative," Kelley said. But in this playfulness, this almost childlike exploration of materials and angles, chicken scratch, and sticky notes, shapes began to form, solutions began building, and the teams could finally see where the project was going. Kelley instructed the teams to take the best of each solution and combine them into the finished product. Each team spent all night manufacturing its parts and assembling them with the other teams.

PRESENTING THE RESULT

The next day the teams presented their solution. The resulting shopping cart was remarkable, both aesthetically and functionally. The familiar, large wire-framed basket was replaced with tracks that held small hand baskets. Members of the shopping team found that the original carts were either competing for aisle space or being left at the end of aisles while the shopper traveled down the aisle to retrieve desired items. So they replaced the large basket reservoir with smaller, mobile versions. This would also reduce theft—another problem they found during discovery. It was common for large basket shopping carts to be stolen and used for everything from laundry carriers to wheelbarrows. Smaller hand baskets would virtually eliminate these uses.

The safety team found that a number of children were being injured by carts every year, so it devised a child seat with a hinged safety arm that could be lowered and a work area for the child to engage

THE IDEO SHOPPING CART CONCEPT

The overarching idea behind the redesign concept was not just to rethink the cart, but to rethink how we shop. IDEO's solution was to solve four problems: shopping, safety, checkout, and wayfinding.

BEHAVIOR OBSERVATIONS

Notice how the large resevoir of the previous design was replaced with a series of nestable hand baskets, allowing the shopper to park the cart and retrieve items by hand.

PERIPHERY SOLUTIONS

Two of the most common complaints among shoppers were the need for price checks in the aisle and the wait time at checkout. IDEO installed a personal scanner on every cart to alleviate price confusion at the shelf and speed checkout.

RESEARCH REVELATIONS

IDEO released the typical front-facing back wheels and replaced them with swivel wheels to provide 360-degree movement around corners and into parkable spaces.

Photos Courtesy of IDEO

in activity. The team also replaced the bottom shelf of the cart where people often stand to ride with a zigzagging structure to allow for the storage of flat items but left no place to stand. In addition, the team designed 360 degree wheels so the cart could be moved sideways if needed, eliminating the need to place your foot on that lower shelf and move the basket around tight corners.

The checkout team observed that customers would touch an item at least twice before the clerk scanned the item for checkout: once when they took it off the shelf and once when they put it on the conveyor belt at checkout. The team built a handheld scanner that attached to the cart so when customers took a product off the shelf, they could scan that item as they put it in the cart and simply provide the checkout clerk with a bill at checkout, greatly decreasing checkout times and all but eliminating pricing questions at the shelf. The item-finding team even built a personal intercom into the handheld checkout scanner to allow customers to ask customer service reps where to find a particular item in the store.

In just five days, IDEO redesigned the common shopping cart to not only better perform the function of a shopping cart, but also to solve a variety of shopping problems in the process and all for roughly the same cost as manufacturing a traditional shopping cart. But this exercise also accomplished something far greater than convenient trips to the grocer. IDEO's Deep Dive process and the resulting shopping cart project offered a unique look into creativity and the creative process, providing a killer example of how you can improve your own creative output. It provided an analogy to the framework for understanding creativity and laid the foundation for basic creative training. In the ensuing chapters, you'll explore the creative basics in detail. But for the sake of summary, the following section presents your Creative Boot Camp Field Guide, the basics of creative training.

CREATIVE BOOT CAMP FIELD GUIDE

After you read about these eight Field Guide topics, you'll begin the Creative Boot Camp Training Program. Understanding these basics will ensure that the time you spend in Creative Boot Camp will be time well spent. Once you have a basic understanding of creative training under your belt, the program will test what you've learned, giving you a practical application for each of these eight principles. A summary of each of the Field Guide topics follows.

1 CREATIVITY IS A HABIT

The basic misconception about creativity is that it is an outside force that you don't control, summon, or affect. The truth is that creativity is not a mystical moment that strikes when you are in the shower. (Why is the shower always the special place of enlightenment? What are you DOING in there?!) Creativity is actually a habit. It is a process that you can affect like you would any other skill—with passion, dedication, and practice.

Society has attached two significant meanings to creativity and neither is true. First, you have been led to believe that "creativity equals gifted." A study out of Exeter University found that even the most "gifted" creatives of all time practiced for years to perform their mastered crafts at levels that would qualify them as "gifted." Second, you have somehow come to the conclusion that "creative equals artistic" when in fact creativity is not a child of the arts; it is problem solving. To practice creative thought, you must first define a problem and then solve it with novelty and relevance. Linda Naiman, author of the book *Orchestrating Collaboration at Work* (BookSurge Publishing, 2007) and founder of the creative coaching alliance Creativity at Work, writes, "Creativity involves two processes: thinking, then producing. If you have ideas, but don't act on them, you are imaginative but not creative."

2 *PURPOSE AND RESTRICTION = CREATIVE FUEL*

If creativity is truly a habit, if it is something that you can affect with practice, what do you practice? Creativity is an innate talent *and* a learned skill. The good news is, according to a rather well-known study performed by NASA in the late 1960s, everyone possesses the innate talent to be creative as a child. The bad news is, as you grew, you were either inadvertently encouraged by figures of authority or trained yourself to be uncreative, but the talent is still there lying dormant, which is where the learned skill comes in. If you give creativity the proper conditions, you can resurrect your creative self and even marry your hibernating creativity with years of perspective and experience to generate ideas you didn't even know you had. What are those conditions? Purpose and restriction.

You cannot be creative without purpose and restriction. They are the only two structural requirements for creative thought. Creativity, at its core, is problem solving. To exercise creativity, you must have a problem to solve. If you paint a beautiful picture but don't solve a problem in doing so, you are being artistic but not creative. A problem must be present for you to apply creative thought; there must be a purpose. Likewise, you must have restrictions in order to be creative. The more restrictive the environment, the greater the opportunity for novelty.

3 *BECOMING AN EPIC FAILURE*

Isaac Newton once wrote, "An essential aspect of creativity is not being afraid to fail." You have all heard that failure is part of the creative process, but evidently, your bosses and authority figures don't seem to subscribe to the same mentality. Creativity is rarely frowned upon by corporate culture, but failure will lead you to a swift kick in the pants and a lonely seat on the curb. Can one exist without the other? The short and long answer is "not on your life."

INTRODUCTION

In this book, you'll explore how to generate ideas in greater quantity and quality. Quality is measured by two attributes: novelty and relevance. By its very nature, novelty is defined as new or original. For something to be new, it can never have existed in its current form before. There is inherent risk with things that are new in that they have never been presented for acceptance or rejection. To produce creative thought, you have to accept novelty as a primary measurement and therefore must be willing to present your ideas for acceptance or rejection. Failure is a natural part of the creative process, as seminal to creative thought as a problem to solve. I would go so far as to say that you cannot be truly creative without a willingness to fail.

4 *PROBLEM SOLVING: BAPTISM BY FIRE*

In the IDEO shopping cart example, you saw a total immersion into the problem. The team broke up into smaller groups and headed out into the world to do research. Their job was to redesign the shopping cart, but they knew that by saturating themselves with what the shopping cart served, not just the cart, they could develop a considerably stronger solution. This is problem baptism by fire, dropping yourself into the problem's environment with the determined intention of developing a perspective that you can use to solve creatively.

You often view creativity's role as providing multiple quality solutions to a given problem, but creativity can also play a part in defining the right problem. IDEO investigated how people shop and solved outer-ring problems from an inner-ring perspective.

5 *SOLVING THE PIECES*

The general perception of problem solving is that there is a simple solution to every problem. Although this may be true for some problems, others are simply too complex for simple solutions. There is nothing wrong with complex solutions to complex problems if those solutions are broken apart and solved on a molecular level. This is a by-product of problem baptism by fire. Inevitably, you find that simple problems are actually complex problems summarized. To effectively solve the shopping cart problem, IDEO separated the project into four smaller problems. The team solved those smaller problems first and then brought the solutions together to solve the greater problem.

The benefit to the mentality of problem dissection is that the philosophy and process work for almost all problems, simple or complex. Learn to divide and conquer, and the skill will serve you in most problem-solving situations, but the skill is not easily learned. You have become accustomed to providing answers not solutions. Yes, there is a difference. Answers are definite, resolute, and most of the time, singular. Solutions, however, are abstract, fluctuating, and subjective. How did you unlearn creativity? You were trained that there is one right answer for every question, and if you didn't know it, you were wrong. Innovation demands that you put aside the common perception of that one right answer for an infinite supply of possibilities. These possibilities are complex, and to arrive at them, you must learn how to solve the pieces.

6 PLAY IS THE NEW WORK

Kevin Carroll, famed Creative Katalyst and author of *Rules of the Red Rubber Ball* (ESPN, 2005), says that creativity and play share a host of common characteristics: There's an inherent positive mind-set, you're driven toward a purpose, the mind can freely wander, consequences are minimized, and it's fun. Think about playing a game. In the midst of that game, you have a goal (winning), you have restrictions (the rules), there are minimal consequences (no one gets fired or dies, usually), and the intention is entertainment; you're playing it because it is fun. These are the ideal circumstances for creative thought. Imagine the ideas you would generate if you knew you would never fail. This is the reason play is an essential aspect of creative training and why the exercises you will undertake during the program are meant to be playful.

The common misconception about play is that it is frivolous. Carroll says, "Play is not always frivolous; there is strategic play. In the midst of play there has to be this inventiveness—this problem solver, this abstract thinker—there has to be this amazing ability to take risk, which are all the things we are asked to do in a business setting." There's another entity that mirrors these same characteristics: improv. Improvisers must throw aside self-critique, fear, and consequence to take risks, be bold, and think quickly. If you can learn to do the same thing in your creative life, you will see significant creative growth.

7 OVERCOMING THE OBSTACLES

In every pursuit, there are obstacles. Your pursuit is to make creativity a habit. The creating or breaking of any habit is never easy. There are always walls erected in your path. If you're trying to create the habit of healthy living through diet, the obstacles of chocolate cake in the fridge and a rumbling stomach at 2:30 in the afternoon may keep you from creating that habit. Likewise, if you want to develop the habit of thinking creatively, you must first identify the obstacles that keep you from achieving that habit and then devise your plan to circumvent them.

In football, the defensive linemen are there for one purpose: to stop the offense's advance. They are a virtual wall of behemoths who are bent on stopping the ball carrier. In goal-line situations, the offense has a couple of options to thwart this formidable obstruction: go around them, go under them, or go over them. Jumping the linemen is an athletic move best performed by players who are willing to hurl their bodies as human missiles over the contingent of giants trying to stop them. As creatives, you must first identify the various obstacles (the linemen) that will keep you from developing the habit of creative thought and then be willing to jump the line in an impassioned act of determination. And you have to be willing to do it over and over when it inevitably fails.

8 *MEASURING CREATIVITY*

Because creativity is typically viewed as an apparition, an uncatchable entity that bestows brilliance upon a fortunate few at indiscriminate times, most have never attempted to measure it. But if creativity is a habit and if it is a process you can control, there certainly must be a unit of measurement in which to gauge your progression. For the purposes of this program, yours will be quantity and quality.

The quantity of the ideas you generate are easy enough to determine: Provide the purpose of a problem and the restriction of time, and you have a usable method. Quality, on the other hand, is a human determination. Relevance is difficult to measure resolutely because the quality of an idea is as subjective as the individual judging it. But relevance is only half the equation. Novelty is also in play when you determine the quality of an idea, so you'll use this attribute to gauge your progress through this journey. If you train to generate more novel ideas and do so over an extended period of time, you will make a habit of creativity.

This is the Creative Boot Camp Field Guide—eight principles that make up the habit of creativity and provide a framework for practicing creative thought. Now let's set your creative baseline with your first Creative Boot Camp exercise.

PRE-TEST

The *Creative Boot Camp* program features a series of daily creative exercises designed to prepare you to generate ideas in greater quantity and quality. At the conclusion of each week, you will be encouraged to complete a progress exercise to gauge your creative growth through the program. As you complete each progress exercise, you can enter your solutions into your personalized Creative Boot Camp dashboard available at www.creativebootcamp.net. The responses will be measured for quality and quantity, and you will receive an updated Creative Growth Score.

To establish your initial Creative Growth Score and your starting rank of Private, take the following Pre-Test and record your responses in the Pre-Test Exercise section of your Creative Boot Camp dashboard at www.creativebootcamp.net.

MEDIEVAL KID'S MEAL

TIME LIMIT: 3 MINUTES

The kid's meal has become a staple of fast-food chains worldwide. A miniaturized meal for children is accompanied by a cheap, useless toy. What could be better? In 1979, the first kid's meal was offered and parents have been stepping on the equivalent of plastic ninja stars ever since. But what if we moved that date back a few 100 years? Your first *Creative Boot Camp* exercise will invite you to find out.

Using a pen or pencil and paper, or a computer, document as many toys as you can conjure up for a kid's meal. But not just any kid's meal; a kid's meal during medieval times. Yes, I mean that era of knights, horses, and castles, the whole nine yards. And you have only three minutes to do it.

CREATIVITY IS A HABIT

Creativity has long been viewed as this "magical divine entity," an uncontrollably fickle daemon that you cannot capture, schedule, or summon despite every effort or desire. Those of you who are *creatives* desperately want to generate ideas in greater quantity and quality, not just for your work but for you. You find value in your ability to generate worthy ideas, and few people would proclaim they are satisfied with their current creative output. Like a killer roller-coaster ride or a fresh, warm chocolate chip cookie, you can't stop at just one experience. You want more.

The challenge then becomes, how do I get more of something I can't control? The answer lies in the errancy of the question. You *do* control it. In fact, creativity is a habit that you can improve through practice. Let's look at the critical myths and truths of creativity.

CREATIVITY, DAEMONS, AND MAGIC

In February 2009, *Eat, Pray, Love* (Penguin Books, 2007) author Elizabeth Gilbert gave a TED talk called "Your Elusive Creative Genius." In it, she tells a story that serves as the foundation to how we, as a collective society, often define creativity.

> *"But, ancient Greece and ancient Rome—people did not happen to believe that creativity came from human beings back then, OK? People believed that creativity was this divine attendant spirit that came to human beings from some distant and unknowable source, for distant and unknowable reasons. The Greeks famously called these divine attendant spirits of creativity 'daemons.' Socrates, famously, believed that he had a daemon who spoke wisdom to him from afar. The Romans had the same idea, but they called that sort of disembodied creative spirit a genius, which is great, because the Romans did not actually think that a genius was a particularly clever individual. They believed that a genius was this, sort of magical divine entity, who was believed to literally live in the walls of an artist's studio—kind of like Dobby the house elf—and who would come out and sort of invisibly assist the artist with their work and would shape the outcome of that work."*

The ancient empires generated many practical ideas, but the perception that creativity manifests itself as a mystical force is not one of them. Creativity is not magic, it's not uncontrollable, and it doesn't strike like lightning when you least expect it. It only seems that way because these moments of brilliance aren't the conscious result of deliberate preparation. Because you did nothing to receive this gifted thought, you consequently believe it must be magic.

Let's look at an example of a standard, scholastic written test. If you studied like mad for the exam, taking every possible measure to retain the information needed to succeed, and then aced the test, no one would deduce that the result of that test was magical or supernatural. Your preparation led to your success. However, remove that preparation and the reasoning changes. If you never consciously studied for the exam and never opened the book or took any notes, and then somehow aced the test, you'd be prone to believe a divine power must have intervened, even if that divine power was sheer dumb luck. If you're like me, you have someone in mind that seemed to experience this divine intervention on a regular basis. And if you're like me, that person was not you.

You believe that creativity is a magical force because you don't recognize any structured preparation leading to the result of a great idea. You assume that the idea simply emerged from thin air because in many instances the idea doesn't materialize after careful thought. Instead, it presents itself in unrelated places at unexpected times.

However, the error is believing that you haven't prepared for that moment at all. The truth is that creativity is innate to everyone. You've been demonstrating the results of this practice since you were a child but doing so at a descending rate. When you are "struck" with a creative idea, it isn't the interference of a mystical power into your perceived normal but rather a brief return to your innate self. It is the residual effect of the systematic degradation of creative thought that has been occurring since childhood.

RELEARNING GENIUS-LEVEL CREATIVITY

In 1968, a general systems scientist named George Land conducted an experiment. He gave 1600 5-year-olds a creativity test that NASA used to determine the level of innovative potential in prospective engineers and scientists. He then reissued the test to those same children when they turned 10 years old and then again when they turned 15. Later, he issued the same creativity test to 280,000 adults. The results were astounding and give validity to the idea that, despite people's admissions to the contrary, everyone is creative.

In the study, 98 percent of 5-year-olds registered genius-level creativity. Anyone who has ever watched a 5-year-old process life can see the truth in that statistic. But then five short years later Dr. Land found that only 30 percent of those same children, now at age 10, registered genius-level creativity. At 15 years old, only 12 percent of those same children met the same level. When the test was administered to adults, the results registered their genius-level creativity at only 2 percent. Dr. George Land concluded that people don't learn to become creative over time or are randomly bestowed the supernatural gift of creativity. Rather, everyone is born creative and actually *unlearn* it.

If creativity is something you can *unlearn*, then logic tells you it is something that you can *relearn*. How can you relearn being creative? Like the written exam analogy, you prepare.

CREATIVITY IS PROBLEM SOLVING

You shouldn't be surprised when an idea seems to come out of thin air because you've been preparing to generate ideas all of your life. When you open the cupboard and make dinner from what you find, you are being creative. When you see traffic stopping on the freeway ahead and you get off to take an alternate route, you are being creative. When a file won't open on your computer and you find a way to extract its contents, you are being creative. You engage in creative thought every day, often failing to recognize the creative output as the result of preparation. Creativity isn't a magical force; creativity is a habit that you've been inadvertently building for most of your life.

Creativity is problem solving. It has special requirements and necessary conditions, but at its core, it is a process. Every problem you solve, you've done so by applying some level of creativity. Common solutions require only a low level of creativity, whereas novel solutions require higher levels.

If the problem you face is unlocking the door to your house with an arm full of groceries during a rainstorm, you could say that putting down the groceries on the wet porch and unlocking the door is a low-level creative thought. The problem was solved (unlocking the door), but the solution lacked novelty (you now have a wet grocery bag and the potential for a mess if it tears). However, keeping the groceries in your arms and punching the code of the electronic garage door opener into the external keypad with your nose would demonstrate a higher level of creative thought. The problem was solved and done so with a degree of novelty.

INCREASING THE QUANTITY OF IDEAS

Because you solve all types of problems on a daily basis, you are inadvertently practicing creative thought and preparing to generate novel ideas. If your intention is to generate ideas in greater quantity and quality, increasing your ability to generate worthwhile ideas when you need them, your goal should be to purposefully and deliberately solve problems and do so with an escalating degree of novelty. By learning to taper the critic within you, you practice generating quantity. By consciously escalating the degree of novelty, you practice generating quality.

In her book *InGenius* (HarperOne, 2012), author Tina Seelig recounts the results of a brain research study designed to discover what occurs in the brain when practicing creatives are engaged in ideation:

> *"Preliminary brain research by Charles Limb at Johns Hopkins University shows that the parts of your brain that are responsible for self-monitoring are literally turned off during creative endeavors. He uses functional magnetic resonance imaging (MRI), which measures metabolic activity in the different areas of the brain, to study brain activity in jazz musicians and rap artists. While they are in the MRI scanner, he asks the musicians to compose an improvisational piece of music.*
>
> *While they are playing, Limb has found that a part of the brain's frontal lobes believed to be responsible for judgment shows much lower activity. This implies that during this creative process the brain actively shuts off its normal inhibition of new ideas. For many activities it is important to have high self-monitoring of your behavior so that you don't say everything you think or do everything that you consider. But when you are generating new ideas, this function gets in the way. Creative people have apparently mastered the art of turning off this part of their brains to let their ideas flow more smoothly, unleashing their imagination."*

The study highlights a key in training yourself to generate ideas in greater quantity: self-critique. As Seelig points out, it is important to have a healthy filter for your behavior to avoid putting yourself in situations you will later (or immediately) regret. Ideation thrives when you taper that filter during idea generation. By learning to "flip the switch" on self-critique, you are more open to generating a greater number of ideas.

Consider the earlier problem of getting into your locked house with an arm full of groceries during a rainstorm. As you stand on the front porch, you have two apparent paths to take: solutions that keep the groceries in your arms and solutions that involve setting the groceries down on the wet porch. Self-critique during ideation may lead you to decide that any solution that puts the groceries on the wet porch is unacceptable and should be avoided. You are then left with only solutions that keep the groceries in your arms. This results in one obvious solution: You need to reposition and balance the groceries in your arms to get the keys from your pocket to unlock the door without spilling the groceries across the porch.

Now flip the switch. By removing self-critique and instant idea evaluation, you start to quickly brainstorm solutions. Two paths still exist; nothing is off the table yet. Putting the paper bag on the wet porch will certainly get the bag wet, but there are options if you go this route: You could lay something dry on the porch and set the bag on that, put the bag in something else to protect it, or set the bag down on your shoes for a moment until you unlock the door. You're standing on the porch, but that's not the only entrance to your home. You could enter through the garage if you can punch in the code on the external panel. You could also put the groceries down on the dry back porch and enter there, or perhaps hang the groceries on the fence while you open the side door. By removing the self-critique that naturally comes as you evaluate the ideas you generate, you can produce a greater quantity of ideas.

Not all of these ideas may be worthy, but you can evaluate worth once you have a greater collection to review. If you had just stood on the front porch, self-critiqued, and only considered ideas that solved the problem from that perspective, you never would have had a chance to generate the idea that led to a more creative solution.

EXPECTATIONS AND EDUCATION

Training yourself to remove self-critique isn't easy, because you've been conditioned to believe that there is only one right answer to every question. From simple parental expectation (when your parents asked you what sound a dog makes, they expected you to answer "ruff!" even though a dog makes a variety of sounds) to formal education, it was ingrained in you that there is an approved answer to every question and that alternative answers were not part of the curriculum. The measures of success in academic systems were built upon the frequency with which you retained and produced these singular answers. Creativity and the possibility of multiple solutions to problems were systematically removed from your public perceptions of success, namely academic, as you reached higher levels of education.

Sir Ken Robinson, renowned education expert and author of *The Element* (Penguin Books, 2009), once said:

> "Every education system on earth has the same hierarchy of subjects. Every one. Doesn't matter where you go. You'd think it would be otherwise, but it isn't. At the top are mathematics and languages, then the humanities, and the bottom are the arts. Everywhere on Earth. And in pretty much every system too, there's a hierarchy within the arts. Art and music are normally given a higher status in schools than drama and dance. There isn't an education system on the planet that teaches dance every day to children the way we teach them mathematics...Truthfully, what happens is, as children grow up, we start to educate them progressively from the waist up. And then we focus on their heads. And slightly to one side."

Robinson contends that the permission to be wrong is stripped away, and with it, creativity. "If you're not prepared to be wrong, you'll never come up with anything original." If you're willing to be wrong and taper your own self-critique, you will generate ideas in greater quantity. They may not all be of value, but you're assured that you'll never generate original ideas that have value if you're not willing to generate original ideas that don't.

INCREASING THE QUALITY OF IDEAS

Quantity, however, isn't your only goal. You also want to increase the quality of your ideas. To do this, you first have to identify what defines quality. The quality of an idea is a very human measurement. It is typically based on two qualifications: how thoroughly does it solve the problem and how novel is the solution. Both are subjective measures but can be quantified through a series of filters. When evaluating how well a solution solves a problem, you gauge success in terms of restrictions overcome. In the earlier groceries example, there were three criteria: 1) Did you get in the house? 2) Did you get the bag wet? and 3) How quickly and easily did you accomplish the task? If a solution enables you to say that you got in the house without the bag getting wet and in very little time, you would view that solution as successful. It met the first qualification, but the level of creativity demonstrated by the solution has yet to be determined. If the manner in which you met this qualification was not readily apparent or required an unusually unique process to accomplish, the second qualification would be met and you would say that the solution demonstrated a higher level of creativity.

Practicing the act of meeting the first qualification alone will not improve your ability to generate ideas in greater quality. You may see an increase in the speed in which you solve problems, but the creativity levels of those solutions will see little improvement because you will draw only upon the obvious solutions in an effort to see any viable solution meet the problem, novel or not. Novelty defines the level of creativity inherent to a solution. It is novelty that you must include as you practice problem solving if you want to boost the creativity levels of the solutions you generate.

PRACTICING NOVELTY WITH RELEVANCE

The challenge with practicing novelty comes in ensuring relevance. The dictionary defines creativity as "the ability to transcend traditional ideas and to create meaningful new ideas." The key adjectives in that description are "meaningful" and "new." It's considerably easier to generate novel ideas if those ideas aren't saddled with the pressure of relevance, but without relevance an idea cannot be creative. Problem solving has that pesky little condition that the problem has to actually be solved. The degree by which it gets solved defines relevance. New for new's sake is not creative.

For instance, you could have solved the grocery-carrying, house-entering problem by blowing the door to splinters with an RPG. This is certainly a novel approach, and most people wouldn't have solved that problem with military-grade artillery. But the solution wasn't terribly relevant because after entering the home with the groceries, you would be confronted with an entry reminiscent of war-torn Europe. The solution was new but not meaningful.

So how do you practice novelty and relevance when you're solving problems? You take small steps. If you were going to run a marathon, you wouldn't sign up six months in advance, do nothing to prepare or train, and then show up the day of the event and start sprinting the moment the starter's gun fired. This would not end well. It may not even start well. To survive 26.2 miles, you must build up endurance, which you do over time. You start by running short distances until your body builds an expectation of accomplishment. Then you build up to the race by increasing the distances you run during the training period prior to the race. Each distance you run builds into the next until your body has been conditioned to survive the totality of the challenge that awaits.

Training to generate ideas in greater quality requires the same type of buildup. Start by solving problems that first demonstrate relevance and build the novelty measurement over time. Move from expected, obvious solutions to those that are a little further from the norm until you're able to discern obvious from novel on the fly. *Creative Boot Camp* will provide opportunities throughout the program for you to up the novelty quotient in your ideas by providing problems that challenge you to start with the obvious and end with the novel. By the end of the program, your initial ideas should become more novel. Through the process, you'll increase your level of creative output, which will lead you to build ideas of greater quality.

THE WRAP

By solving problems regularly, flipping the switch on your self-critique, and doing so with an increase in novelty and relevance, you will develop the habit of creative thought. This habit will lead you to instinctively generate ideas in greater quantity and quality when you desire, and sometimes even when you don't. As many will attest to, turning the ideator off is more difficult than turning it on. If you enjoy hours of restful sleep with little to no problem reaching REM states of blissful slumber, it may behoove you to stop reading this book. There's a cost to generating ideas in greater quantity and quality: The faucet keeps running long after you've turned off the knob. The brain has a way of deciding on its own when it is done.

Next, you'll investigate the only two conditions needed to produce creative thought: purpose and restriction. These two conditions become the foundation for the exercises you will perform throughout the program.

PURPOSE AND RESTRICTION = CREATIVE FUEL

Two conditions must exist for creativity to be possible: purpose and restriction. A problem (purpose) needs solving, and an obstacle or obstacles need to be overcome to solve it (restrictions). Without both conditions, creativity is not possible. One cannot live without the other, and the severity of either provides the fertile ground needed for creativity to thrive.

There is an implicit third condition that must also exist for creativity to be present: action. From problem design to idea fulfillment, action ensures that you are keeping the core "create" in "creative."

DUNCKER'S CANDLE PROBLEM

In 1945, Clark University Gestalt psychologist Karl Duncker published a cognitive performance test known as *Duncker's Candle Problem*. In an effort to measure the influence of functional fixedness (using an object in only the way it was designed to be used) on a participant's problem-solving capabilities, Duncker gave test participants three objects: a candle, a box of thumbtacks, and a book of matches. He then gave them these instructions: Fix a lit candle to the wall in a way so that the candle won't drip wax on the floor or table below.

It's easy to see the creative possibilities in this exercise. Duncker had what he deemed as "the solution" in mind, and he wanted to see if his test participants could do the one thing they'd need to do to solve the problem: see the box of tacks as multiple objects, not just one. Specifically, he wanted to see how many participants would see and use the actual box. The solution that he designed was to empty the cardboard box of thumbtacks, tack the box to the wall, and place the lit candle in the box. The cognitive bias of functional fixedness infers that people are conditioned to see and use objects for their primary purpose only. Therefore, seeing the box as a separate and usable instrument rather than just a carrier of thumbtacks was the real challenge he was testing.

Some attempted to partially melt the candle in an effort to create an adhesive that could be used to fix the candle to the wall (unsuccessfully). Others developed alternative and considerably more direct methods of tacking the candle to the wall (again, unsuccessfully). Few were able to produce the solution Duncker was expecting.

In subsequent studies, alterations to the conditions were introduced to test their effects on reaching the intended solution. Most notably, removing the tacks from the box and presenting the box as a separate object rather than a container for the tacks produced nearly perfect results. Even small changes to the wording of the problem had drastic effects. Presenting the objects as a box *and* tacks rather than a box *of* tacks or underlining the words *candle, box, tacks, book,* and *matches* had a significantly positive effect on the solutions.

Although the exercise was obviously designed to test the effect of functional fixedness, an important lesson should be learned from the test: *Creativity has requirements.*

PURPOSE SETS UP THE PROBLEM

As a characteristic of problem solving, purpose defines the problem. Problems can be as small as a question or as large as a state, but you cannot apply creativity without a problem because it is the purpose. If there is no problem to be solved, there is no creativity.

Take a work of art, for example. If someone paints a beautiful painting, abstract or realistic, colorful or restrained, the result is not creative unless there was a problem to be solved. It is artistic but not creative. Throw in even the smallest of problems, and the same work immediately becomes creative—to what level is still an open variable.

Say the artist paints a portrait of a beautiful woman. If his only goal is to create or re-create beauty, there is no problem being solved because beauty is completely subjective. "How do I make something beautiful?" is not a problem because there is no way to be wrong. However, if that same artist painted the same portrait of the same beautiful woman but did so using only three predefined colors, within a certain style, or without using brushes, the same work would now solve a problem and creativity would be present alongside artistry. A premeditated problem existed that contained premeditated restrictions; therefore, the problem could be solved and done so to a variety of creative degrees.

PROBLEM CONTRACTION AND EXPANSION

Chapter 4 explores problem design, but to understand the idea of purpose, you must grasp a basic understanding of problem contraction and expansion. Every problem can be fine-tuned to provide optimal conditions for creativity to thrive. Some problems need to be contracted, and some problems need to be expanded. As an analogy, think of making balloon animals. To effectively fuse together balloons of different lengths and sizes, balloon animal artists must fill balloons with varying amounts of air. Some balloons are filled halfway to allow for more slack when they tie them to other balloons. Some are filled with more air to expand their shape and stability. Often, balloon animal artists fill balloons and then let out a little air or add a little more air to get the right conditions to fold them into a giraffe or peacock. When you encounter problems that you want to solve with a high degree of creativity, you may need to make small adjustments to the problem to produce the optimal creative conditions.

NARROWING A PROBLEM

You can often broaden the creative opportunity of a solution by narrowing the problem. To some degree, this is an act of tightening restrictions. But a well-defined problem has an infinitely greater chance of being solved creatively than an indistinct one. An example of problem contraction told by *The Seven Lessons* (Paton Professional, 2012) author Craig Cochran is of a little girl who was kept serially awake by the sound of scratching in the attic above her bed. Obviously afraid, she asked her father about the sounds. Her father advised that they both go up to the attic to uncover the source of the sounds. She was understandably reluctant but eventually agreed, and with her father and a pair of flashlights, they ascended to the attic. A brief exploration uncovered a pair of furry tree squirrels that had found their way into the crawl space. Delighted, the little girl and her father returned to her room. "You're not scared anymore?" asked the father. "No," answered the girl, "it's not scary anymore. We know what the problem is. It's not scratching sounds; it's squirrels."

Some of the hardest problems to solve are those defined as "scratching sounds." They elicit the greatest fear because they have no form or shape; they are unknown. You can solve what you know with a greater deftness because you can define the relevance of the solution. Then it is a matter of knowing or defining the restrictions that you must overcome to solve the problem.

BROADENING A PROBLEM

On the flip side, you can also broaden the creative opportunity of a solution by widening the problem. Some problems are so minutely defined that they encourage few possible solutions. Broadening these problems opens up more possibilities, and with more possibilities comes a greater chance at novelty.

At my agency, we asked employees what office improvements they wanted to see. Many of the responses contained versions of, "I'd like to see an awning or cover over the back deck." A deck is attached to the back of the building but isn't covered, so when it rains or snows, the deck is unusable. This problem has little opportunity for a high level of creativity within the solution because the solution has already been defined in the problem. To fine-tune the problem, we gathered the people who had made that request and talked about what they really wanted. We found that they didn't really want a deck cover; instead, they wanted an outdoor space where they could go to escape for a moment. And they wanted to do this with other people to enjoy a beverage or a smoke and talk about topics other than work for a few minutes. With no awning, the back deck could not be used to perform that function year round. But an awning wouldn't protect people from the winter cold either—a factor that few considered when making the request. By widening the problem, we were able to develop ideas in greater quantity and quality, focusing on improving the quality of work life at the agency, not just focusing on the minutiae of a deck covering.

RESTRICTION SETS UP THE SOLUTION

Purpose is the first necessary condition for creativity, but purpose is useless without restriction. Most creatives bemoan restrictions, incorrectly targeting them as the inhibitor of their creative efforts. However, the opposite is actually true. It is not restriction that *prohibits* you from being creative; restriction *enables* you to be creative. Without restriction, creativity can't exist. The degree of novelty that defines the level of creativity within a solution is directly related to the restrictions overcome within that problem.

In the grocery-carrying, house-entering example in Chapter 1, the primary problem was easy to define: get in the house. The restrictions of the problem provide the measurement for creativity: Get in the house *quickly without getting the grocery bag wet.* Getting in the house is easy if those restrictions don't need to be met. Just drop the bag and walk in. Restrictions set the stage for a creative solution.

You've all heard the phrase "think outside the box." This is usually a plea to develop unusual ideas, ideas that aren't of an ordinary nature. Ernie Schenck, author of *The Houdini Solution* (McGraw-Hill, 2006), contends that this "box" is impossible to remove if your goal is to develop creative ideas. He writes that what you need to do is learn to make the box smaller and think *inside* the box. "Limitations are like the banks of a river. Without them, the river becomes instead a formless mass without direction, just sort of spreading out everywhere but going nowhere."

The psychologist Rollo May puts it this way: "Creativity requires limits; for the creative act arises out of the struggle of human beings and against that which limits them."

Now, let's add one more chestnut: The more restrictive the problem, the more creative the solution can become. Restrictions can actually take an ordinary solution and make it creative without changing anything else.

Let's say you've been commissioned to design a new logo for your company. You have 12 months to design the logo and have an unlimited amount of money. You can use as many colors as you like and any shape or form that you desire. In other words, you have a blank canvas.

A year passes since you were awarded the project, and you return with your solution: a black box with the initials of the company knocked out of the box. Did you solve the problem? Yes. Does your solution demonstrate a high level of creativity? No. So let's change the restrictions and try it again.

You are sitting at your desk working on a project that is due in 30 minutes. Your boss comes over to you and says, "I'm so sorry; I totally forgot to tell you that I volunteered you to redesign the company logo. I was supposed to tell you a few months ago, but it slipped my mind. The problem is, the owner of the company is walking toward us. See that spring in his step and smile on his face? The reason he's so happy is because he's coming over here to look at the new logo you've designed. Quick, design something!" In the ten seconds it takes the owner to walk over to you, you create a black box with the initials of the company knocked out of it.

Did that solution solve the problem? Yes. Does it demonstrate a high level of creativity? Actually, yes, considering you had ten seconds to do it, it was for the owner of the company, and you were already stressing about the deadline on your other project. Taking into account the insane restrictions placed on the project, the same solution is viewed in a different creative light.

ACCEPT AND CONQUER

Learning to accept the restrictions of a problem and solve around them is fundamental to creative growth. It is one of the most apparent signs of a mature creative. Let's call it *accept and conquer.* The obstacles overcome play a significant role in any creative solution. Walt Disney, one of the greatest creatives of all time, lived this philosophy. His original theme park, Disneyland, has a myriad of examples of restrictions overcome to produce creative results, often without the public even knowing. The Haunted Mansion attraction is a great example. If you've been to the original Disneyland in Southern California and have been on this ride, you know about the stretching room at the beginning of the ride where the paintings on the wall stretch to reveal creepy counterparts. It is a seminal part of the ride, and one that many visitors remember fondly. It may surprise you to learn that it wasn't in the original plans for the attraction; it was the creative result of accept and conquer.

If you've followed Walt's life, you know he was a big fan of trains. When Disneyland was originally built, it was constructed with the Disneyland train route as the perimeter of the park. When it came time to build the Haunted Mansion, it was supposed to be built right next to the train tracks, which meant there was a restriction on where the ride could expand. To solve this problem, the decision was made to build a major portion of the ride underground. This presented a new problem: getting visitors underground without disconnecting them from the fantasy. For many people, this would have been the point when they threw up their hands and complained to management that it was impossible to solve the problem with these restrictions.

The imagineers at Disneyland chose to accept and conquer. They decided to build an elevator that would take people underground, an elevator disguised as a room that stretches to reveal creepy painting counterparts and a skeleton hanging from the ceiling. The result was so beloved that when Disney built The Magic Kingdom in Orlando, Florida, they included the stretching room, even though there is no need to take visitors underground. The room at The Magic Kingdom stretches up.

CREATE RESTRICTIONS

If novelty and relevance thrive within restriction, it tends to reason that the absence of restriction inhibits creative solutions. In these situations, it is imperative that you, as a problem solver, create restriction. If not enough restriction exists, you must create more. It goes against every fiber of your safety-ensuring being, but the only way you can produce creative solutions is if the restrictions are defined.

If a project has no deadline (like that's ever happened), create one. If there's no budget concern (ditto), invent one. If you can't clearly see how success will be measured, develop it. If the restrictions are too broad, tighten them. You spend a great deal of your creative energy trying to control the outcome variables in an attempt to manipulate what you haven't anticipated that you soften your chances of actually solving the problem with any measure of creativity. You try to buy as much time as you can in case you get busy, get the largest budget you can in case your ideas are expensive, and assign soft measurement analysis and taper expectations to ensure that the idea never is viewed as a "failure." There's an age-old business adage that says, "Underpromise and overdeliver." Creatively speaking, this is a cop-out. If you want to grow creatively, learn to overpromise and overdeliver. Don't be afraid to set meaningful restrictions of deadlines, budgets, measurements, and expectations. You can creatively succeed only with these limitations in place.

THE UNSPOKEN THIRD CONDITION: ACTION

Although purpose and restriction are the fuel that powers creativity, there is an unspoken third condition that creativity needs: action. Thomas Edison once said, "To invent you need a goal, imagination, and a pile of junk." Edison is saying that to be creative, you need purpose, restriction, and action. Ideation without action is imagination. There's nothing wrong with imagination; it is certainly an integral part of the creative formula. But the title of this book isn't *Imagination Boot Camp*. You are training to be more creative, to generate ideas in greater quantity and quality, not just to do so, but to apply them to your clients and your own use.

The root word in "creativity" is "create." Creation is a positive, active process. God didn't just think about creating the universe. He created it. Alexander Graham Bell didn't just imagine the telephone, satisfied with the idea. He created it. William Kellogg wasn't content with his breakfast oatmeal replacement idea. He went out and created Corn Flakes (had to throw that in). Creativity is an act, not a thought. Don't settle for imagination alone; be truly creative and create.

Action as the unspoken third condition of creativity isn't just a plea to make what you imagine. It's also a reminder that your own creative growth is in your hands. If creativity is no longer the uncontrollable mystical entity you originally believed, if it is a habit you can improve, that means it is now on you to do something about it. You are no longer bound to circumstance. You can alter your creative mind-set and improve your chances of generating ideas in greater quantity and quality. But this means you must get out of your comfy office chairs and do it.

THE WRAP

Now that you know the necessary conditions creativity requires, you can say with all certainty that you will fail to meet these conditions on a regular basis. Failure is a natural, essential component of generating ideas in greater quantity and quality. In the next chapter, you'll find out that you cannot be creative if failure is not an option.

BECOMING AN EPIC FAILURE

Imagine if you began every ideation session with this premise: What ideas can I generate that solve the problem but have little to no chance of seeing the light of day? It is common to generate ideas that solve problems and do so with the feasibility of acceptance. But this mind-set can also lead to stale, expected ideas. If you're not generating ideas that have a chance to fail, you're not generating creative ideas.

Failure is not typically a goal that you set for yourself. But if it is the right type of failure, it is a goal that will produce more novel ideas. Build a healthy risk tolerance and you can learn to fail effectively and repeatedly without the sting of heightened consequence.

OVERCOMING THE PERCEPTION OF FAILURE

To help illustrate the common perception of failure, let me start by introducing you to Lewis.

Lewis is an aspiring young inventor and unfortunate orphan. When Lewis meets Wilbur, a young teenager from the future, he convinces Wilbur to take him back to the future with him. Wilbur obliges and introduces Lewis to his oddball family. Wilbur explains that his father is a scientist and an inventor, and that not only did he build the time machine that transported them, but also a host of other inventions. Lewis soon discovers that Wilbur isn't being wholly truthful with him, but not before Lewis has an eye-opening family dinner with the clan, minus Wilbur's father.

At this dinner, Lewis is asked to fix one of the family member's inventions: a peanut-butter-and-jelly shooter. The pressure mounts as the baby of the family becomes impatient and wants his sandwich. Lewis does everything he can to fix the device, but in the end, the device explodes and peanut butter and jelly is strewn everywhere. It is an all too familiar feeling for Lewis, this untimely and public failure. But much to his surprise, the family is not upset or disappointed. In fact, they cheer his epic failure. It seems that the patriarch of the family is actually a grown-up Lewis, and his personal motto, *Keep moving forward*, is the family's mantra as well. Failure is not only accepted in this household, it is encouraged.

Lewis isn't real. Actually, Lewis is a character in the 2007 Disney animated feature *Meet the Robinsons*. In the film, Lewis discovers that failure is to be sought after, not avoided. He realizes that you learn more from failure than you do from success.

Lewis isn't alone in his perception of failure. When you begin a project, you don't start by saying, "Man, I sure hope this idea goes down in a fiery ball of carnage and schrapnel."

But imagine if you did?

When asked what advice she would give to student designers about to enter the industry, Sterling Brands Design Division President Debbie Millman said, "I would ask them what they would do if they knew they would never fail, and then I would tell them to do that." The same could be applied to creativity. Imagine the ideas you could produce if you weren't afraid of the consequences. The fact is, the single greatest paralytic barrier to creativity is fear. What are you afraid of?

FEAR OF CHOICE

Nobody wants to be wrong; you avoid it like the plague. Decisions that could lead to wrong are almost immediately disregarded; you take the paths you know, even if the alternatives offer the chance at better. In a natural effort to sustain, you most often choose the known over the unknown because the known is rarely wrong. This is a primal instinct, and one that leads most people to identify and weigh what they have to lose rather than what they have to gain. You tell yourself that it is better to be neutral than to risk being wrong.

FEAR OF JUDGMENT

If you choose to, you can point the finger at every manner of personal experience or influence to explain how you behave. You can blame your parents for how you look, the education system for what you know, and society for how you act. However, the one thing you can't blame on any external entity is the way you think. Your ideas are uniquely yours; they are the most personal and intimate offerings you have. When you are asked to put your ideas on a table, you are laying down your souls for the world to see—and judge. This is a frightening act and one you are careful to perform.

You would rather keep your ideas to yourself than risk the validity of how you think exposed to judgment.

FEAR OF CONSEQUENCE

In poker, there's a betting theory called *pot odds*. The theory is that if there's enough money in the pot, a play that would normally be considered too risky becomes less risky because the reward is much higher. If you need a particular card and the odds are that you have only a 10 percent chance of getting that card, you should probably fold. But if winning the pot would get you ten times the bet you would have to make to take a card and see, the reward is worth the risk. As creatives, you are constantly weighing the risk of an idea versus the reward. In most cases, you are resolved to play it safe because you are afraid of the consequences. If failure had no consequences, no one would fear it. Failure is defined by its consequences. You love play because play carries little consequence. You can fail without fear of losing your job, getting reprimanded by an authority figure, or forfeiting the trust of your coworkers. If you generate an idea and then act on that idea and it fails, you view the risk as outweighing the reward.

These fears exist because creativity is inherently risky. It encourages a steadily increasing level of novelty. Novelty, by definition, means new, and new is always risky. No one knows how new will be received by others, so your instincts are to stay the course. This is known as routine, and routine is the antithesis of creativity.

Creative growth requires that you suspend your fear of failure in order to find novelty in your ideas. If fear keeps you from investigating unexplored creative territory, your ideas are limited to what you currently know. You must be willing to fail in order to succeed. The trick is learning to fail correctly, a skill known well to those who have studied the modern Japanese martial art of Judo.

Judo focuses on throwing an opponent to the ground through grappling maneuvers and takedowns. The moves are complex and rely heavily on manipulating your opponent's weight distribution to gain an advantage. Despite the complexity of the attack maneuvers, a third of most practice sessions are devoted to *ukemi*, which is the art of breaking falls. Masters teach students how to fall to alleviate the risk of injury during an attack. After all, you can't get up swinging if you can't get up.

Learning to fail properly is creativity's version of *ukemi*. If you take more risks in your creative work, you'll experience more failure, but it will help you to understand how to fail correctly. You must first redefine failure, assigning a new focus. Then you must understand the difference between smart failure and dumb failure. In addition, you'll want a practical plan to build your risk tolerance.

REDEFINING FAILURE

Famed designer Milton Glaser was asked his perspective on the fear of failure. He hypothesized that creatives are not really afraid to fail; rather, they are afraid that failure will reveal their true creative limitations—not to others but to themselves. His advice: Embrace failure. Embrace that you are not as good as you want to be, and failure will no longer have the same stigma or sting. Glaser's point is to redefine failure. By viewing failure as a means to an end, in this case personal enlightenment, you will no longer see it as an impediment to success.

Failure is often viewed as the opposite of success. The fear of failing is really the fear of not succeeding. This makes sense. Creatively speaking, however, this presents a conundrum. The problem with that statement is that to succeed creatively, to generate truly creative ideas that are novel and relevant, you must risk failure in order to succeed. This means you must change your perspective of failure from the fear of being wrong to the fear of missing right.

Baba Shiv, professor of marketing at Stanford's Graduate School of Business, coined two terms that describe how people view failure: the type 1 mind-set and the type 2 mind-set:

> *"The type 1 mind-set is fearful of making mistakes. It characterizes most individuals, managers, and corporations today. In this mind-set, to fail is shameful and painful. Because the brain becomes very risk averse under this line of thinking, innovation is generally nothing more than incremental. You don't get off-the-charts results.*
>
> *The type 2 mind-set is fearful of losing out on opportunities. Places like Silicon Valley and the Stanford Graduate School of Business are full of type 2s. What is shameful to these people is sitting on the sidelines while someone else runs away with a great idea. Failure is not bad; it can actually be exciting. From so-called 'failures'*

emerge those valuable gold nuggets—the 'aha!' moments
of insight that guide you toward your next innovation.

We generally start out with the type 2 adventurous spirit
as children. But then somewhere along the line, often
in school, we are squelched. Failure is not allowed. We
become type 1s."

To integrate failure into the creative process, you have to build and maintain a type 2 mind-set. If the possibility that you will miss out on something great is a stronger motivation than the fear that you will be wrong, you are able to generate ideas that have greater novelty and relevance, and consequently, a higher level of creative quality.

IDENTIFY AND EMPLOY SMART FAILURE

Not all failure is created equal. There is dumb failure and there is smart failure. Dumb failure is the result of laziness, ego, and ignorance. Smart failure is the result of maturity, humility, and understanding. Dumb failure happens late in the creative process when there is little time to explore options. This is called *the pridefall.* Smart failures happen early in the creative process when you can apply the knowledge from the failure to the next iteration. This is called *rapid prototyping.*

Animation movie studio Pixar knows a thing or two about creativity. President and cofounder Ed Catmull sees rapid prototyping as an iterative process with risk minimized through a build of sequential prototypes, each slightly more complex than the previous. This provides an early look at ideas to gauge their failure quotient. "In the early stage of making a movie, we draw storyboards…and then edit them together with dialogue and temporary music…The first versions are very rough, but they give a sense of what the problems are…We then iterate; each version typically gets better and better."

CHAPTER 3

As you generate ideas, you should be periodically entering the domain of the unknown. In these instances, it is imperative for you to prototype the unknowns quickly to give you time to either improve the idea or develop an alternative. This is smart failure, quarantining failure to the beginning of the process so you can apply the education that naturally results.

Despite your best efforts, however, you can't segregate all failure to the front of your process. There will be times when failure is in the final execution of an idea. In these instances, you'll want to bury your head in the sand and hide. But mature creatives discover that they can't learn from what they don't experience. If you embrace failure as a natural part of the creative process, you should want to learn as much from the failure as you can so you can apply that knowledge to the next project. These are often referred to as *postmortems*.

Accounting brand Intuit regularly holds "failure parties" to celebrate what was gained through failed product launches and destigmatize the outcome from the intent. Bloomberg *Businessweek* magazine writer Jena McGregor detailed Intuit's progressive perspective in a July 2006 article:

> *"The company had never targeted young tax filers before, and in early 2005, it tried to reach them through an ill-fated attempt to combine tax-filing drudgery with hip-hop style. Through a Web site called RockYourRefund. com, Intuit offered young people discounts to travel site Expedia and retailer Best Buy, and the ability to deposit tax refunds directly into prepaid Visa cards issued by hip-hop mogul Russell Simmons.*
>
> *But even hip-hop stars can't make 1040s cool enough to get young adults excited about taxes. 'We did very few*

returns' through the site, says Rick Jensen, vice president for product management at Intuit's consumer tax group. 'It was almost a rounding error.' Through a postmortem process, the team that developed the campaign documented its insights, such as the fact that Gen Yers don't visit destination Web sites that feel too much like advertising. Then, on a stage at the Dolce Hayes Mansion in San Jose, Calif., last October in front of some 200 Intuit marketers, the team received an award from Intuit Chairman Scott Cook. 'It's only a failure if we fail to get the learning,' said Cook."

Regardless of whether your employers would be open to the idea of "failure parties," the question becomes, "are you?" Do you celebrate failure in the same way you celebrate success? If the failures you experience are smart failures, you absolutely should.

BUILD RISK TOLERANCE

It will take more than a few pages in a book to change your perspective from safety first to participating in failure parties. Building risk tolerance takes time. Think of it like learning to ski. The first time you latch waxed fiberglass to your feet and head out onto nature's slickest surface, your risk tolerance is pretty low. You aren't thinking about thrill; you're thinking about survival. The first thing any instructor teaches isn't how to ski; it's how to stop skiing. This knowledge proves fruitful as you slide down the preschool slope unscathed. You then progress through the educational system of runs, and in time, you're at the top of a mogul-peppered grad school path with a goggle-interrupted sunburn and a grin a mile wide. Your failures at this stage will be more significant but so, too, will the reward. Your risk tolerance is peaking. Building creative risk tolerance takes a similar scaled approach.

In Chapter 7, you'll discover the common obstacles that keep you from growing creatively. One of these battles is called *Pushed Forward vs. Pulled Back*. The basic premise is that you spend most of your ideation creating ideas that need to be pushed forward on the risk scale rather than ideas that need to be pulled back. The first step in building creative risk tolerance is developing the habit of generating even a few ideas that require being pulled back. To do this, you have to find the relevance barrier in the problem you are trying to solve and *purposely* cross it. You don't have to cross it for every idea, but give yourself permission to dance back and forth between what is relevant and what is folly.

For example, recall the grocery-carrying, house-entering problem from Chapter 1. The relevance line is clearly drawn around ideas that get you into the house quickly with a dry grocery bag. The rational boundary around that relevance is destruction. During ideation, you may generate ideas like opening the garage or finding an open window—all relevant ideas. Try mixing in ideas that cross the relevance line, like throwing the groceries through the window or digging a tunnel from the front lawn to the kitchen floor. By mixing in relevance-crossing ideas, you begin to raise your risk tolerance and will begin to generate ideas that reevaluate and redefine the relevance line, opening the door to greater novelty.

Renowned designer, author, and journalist Steven Heller, in his book *Design Disasters: Great Designers, Fabulous Failure, and Lessons Learned* (Allworth Press, 2008), writes:

> "For all the talk of the value of learning through failure, it is difficult to get the concept across if we continue to use the word 'failure' in that sentence. People have a natural aversion to the term, and it is next to impossible to reclaim it for pedagogic purposes."

THE WRAP

To grow creatively, failure, or whatever synonym you apply, must be part of your process. Until it is, you are doomed to live in routine and resolved to miss the fruits of innovation. In the next chapter, you'll explore what it means to immerse yourself in the problem you are trying to solve. Creating an experiential perspective of the problem often reveals untapped creative opportunity.

PROBLEM SOLVING: BAPTISM BY FIRE

The phrase *baptism by fire* comes from an early 19th century French expression that described a soldier's first experience in battle. It literally means to immerse yourself completely in a new experience. As with problem solving, there is no easing into it, no baby steps, and no getting your feet wet. Solving problems with novelty and relevance requires a deep understanding of the problem. It is a step that is commonly overlooked in an effort to execute a solution, and one you may find underdefined in your process. It also requires that you remain willing to redefine the problem if it is too big or too small.

This is known as problem design, and it is a fundamental component of creativity. Effective problem design teaches you to see the inherent stages existent in problems and provides context to solve them creatively.

STAGING THE PROBLEM

Problem design is a broad topic to say the least. There is no universal process to properly design a problem; it is an act of individualization based on a goal. Your goal is to generate ideas in greater quantity and quality, so let me provide an analogy for problem design that will help you accomplish that goal: *Dante's Inferno* will set the stage for a problem design process you can use to incite creative solutions, a process I call *The Pickle*.

The story of Dante's Inferno starts in the late 13th century and takes place in Florence, Italy, which was a political mess at the time. Religious clerics and Roman rule were fighting for power. Like many wealthy Italians, poet Dante Alighieri took sides—and lost. During his exile and in his angst, he did what any person would have done in the same situation (tongue firmly placed in cheek): He penned a series of books that made an intellectual and artistic political allegory of hell. He called the writings *The Comedy*, not because they were funny, but because they had a tragic beginning and a happy ending. In the 16th century, the word *Divine* was added to the title to communicate the obvious religious implication of the work. *The Divine Comedy* became Dante's masterpiece collection, illustrating his metaphorical journey through hell.

One book in particular details the underworld as a series of circles or stages, a tiered justice system for sinners. The more sinister the sinner (from Dante's perspective), the deeper into the circles of hell the sinner was sent. Despite the horror he depicted within the circles, the story was actually one of hope as Dante traveled through these stages of hell to get to heaven. You may know the story as *Dante's Inferno*.

Dante details multiple circles of hell, with each circle becoming increasingly severe as Dante matches the theoretical punishment with the perceived crime. You can imagine how deeply Dante had to go mentally and spiritually to detail such a place, dividing the *Inferno* into specific stages to tell the story of each one. Within this proverbial *baptism by fire* exists an analogy for problem design and creative growth.

Like the degree of specificity found in Dante's circles, every problem you attempt to solve has stages of definition. As you dive deeper into Dante's circles, the focus is more specific. He divided the concept of hell into stages with broad punishments occupying the outer circles and more specific punishments occupying the inner circles. Problem design can be thought of in the same way. You can divide a problem into stages and choose to solve the broad problem occupying the outer circles or the specific problem occupying the inner circles. These degrees provide a mechanism to discover the best opportunity for creative solutions. Although the initial problem you try to solve may be occupying the right stage, you may find that it is inherently flawed and you need to define and solve a problem occupying a different stage.

RECOGNIZING FLAWED PROBLEMS

If creativity is problem solving, then defining the problem is of the utmost importance to solving it creatively. Most problems with which you are confronted are posed *to* you, not *by* you. Someone or something *gives* you the problem, and you solve it—unless, of course, you want to apply a level of creativity to the solution and could benefit from redesigning the problem.

The following are all hyper-specific problems you could solve:

- *"I'd like bigger cabinets in the kitchen."*
- *"We need a brochure for our new product."*
- *"What kind of banner ads will get the most clicks?"*

These problems have obvious if not singular solutions: install bigger cabinets, go with the tri-fold, and produce an animated ad, respectively. But are these solutions creative? Not terribly. The solutions are obvious because they are baked into the problem. However, the issue isn't with the solutions; it's with the problems. They are too acute to solve with much novelty despite the obvious relevance. To do that, you need to immerse yourself in the problem, define the various stages, and choose the stage that presents the most effective problem to solve. I call this process *The Pickle*.

INTRODUCING THE PICKLE

Dante had his *Inferno*, you have *The Pickle*. A pickle is a problem, as in "I'm in a pickle!" *The Pickle* is *the* problem—the unnamed, undefined issue you're trying to solve creatively. Like *Dante's Inferno*, *The Pickle* presents tiered stages of definition. Place the problem you are solving in the stage of *The Pickle* that best defines its specificity, outline the other stages, and then choose the stage that presents the *real* problem, the one that can be solved with the greatest combination of novelty and relevance.

As you can see in the diagram, *The Pickle* presents four stages of problem design. Each stage provides creative opportunities, but the middle stages typically produce the brightest prospects. The innermost stage provides the obvious solutions, whereas the outermost stage presents the biggest picture. The primary goal with any problem is to place it in the right stage of *The Pickle*.

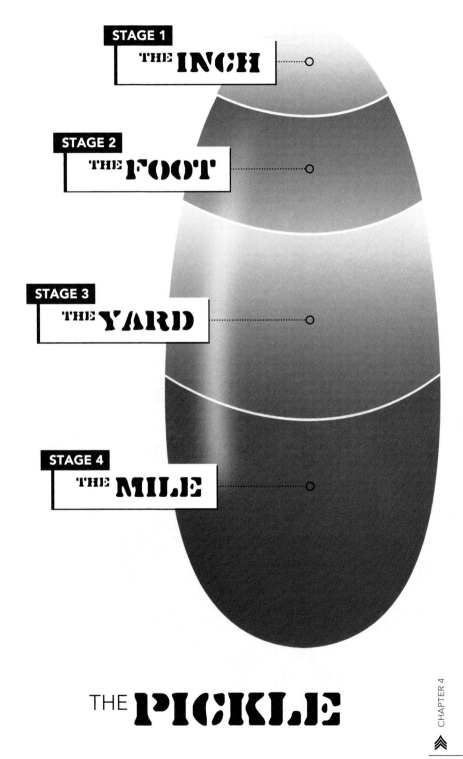

STAGE 1
THE **INCH**

STAGE 2
THE **FOOT**

STAGE 3
THE **YARD**

STAGE 4
THE **MILE**

THE **PICKLE**

Recall in Chapter 2 that I described a problem we faced at my agency. In response to the question "What improvement would you like to see around the agency?", many of the employees asked if we could build a deck cover over the outdoor deck that extended from the rear of the building. After immersing ourselves in the problem, we discovered that the problem presented to us 1) wasn't the problem that needed to be solved and 2) didn't present the greatest opportunity for novelty and relevance. We needed to place the problem we were presented into the proper stage of The Pickle.

Each stage of The Pickle can be expressed as distances from the inevitable solution in the same way that we use the phrase "30,000-foot view" to describe a summary perspective or the term "molecular" to describe a hyper-detailed evaluation. You can place your problem on any stage of The Pickle, but outlining the remaining stages requires a relational view.

THE FOUR STAGES OF THE PICKLE

Stage 1: The Inch ├────┤

Stage 1 is the most common problem you encounter because it is usually presented with some shade of solution wrapped in the quandary. The solutions typically implied in Stage 1 problems may ultimately be appropriate, but in this form there is no opportunity to explore alternatives in an effort to validate them.

In the deck-cover Pickle, the problem defined for this stage was the original problem posed, *How can we build a cover for the deck?*

Stage 2: The Foot ├────────┤

Stage 2 is the face-to-face evaluation of the problem, the detailed view that provides clarity and a natural filter for any solution applied to any of the problems in any other stage. Stage 2 solutions typically provide the greatest balance between novelty and relevance but are still focused on elements of execution or provide some detail of restriction.

In the deck-cover Pickle, the problem defined for this stage was, *How can we integrate a year-round outdoor space for times when employees need to escape and recharge?*

Stage 3: The Yard |————————————————|

Stage 3 is the arms-distance perspective of the problem. It is close enough to see the nuance but far enough away to see the bigger picture. Along with Stage 2, this stage typically represents the most fertile soil for creative solutions but also yields the greatest risk of sacrificing relevance for novelty because the problem is still fairly open.

In the deck-cover Pickle, the problem defined for this stage was, *How can we encourage more agency socialization and collaboration?*

Stage 4: The Mile |———————————————————————————|

Stage 4 is the mile-high view of the problem, the broadest problem you can solve without losing the soul of the problem at hand. This is usually the most difficult to define because it is the furthest away from a tangible, measurable solution. Stage 4 presents the problem that has the most possible solutions because the problem is overtly broad. There is ample opportunity for novelty and little for true relevance.

In the deck-cover Pickle, the problem defined for this stage was, *How do we improve the quality of work life?*

You can see that Stages 2 and 3 are the sweet spots for creative solutions with novelty and relevance but require some work to define the right problem.

DECONSTRUCTING THE PICKLE

There are two key details to note about the stages of The Pickle.

First, each of the problems designed for each stage start with the word *how*. It is a powerful word that rarely implies a solution and encourages a thoughtful response. Framing problems to begin with *how* isn't a hard-and-fast rule, but it represents a solid first step to effective problem design.

Second, you can fill out the stages by working outward or inward. If you start with a Stage 1 question, you can ask, "What is the larger question that this answers?" This provides the context for the next stage. If you start with a Stage 4 question, you can ask, "What are possible answers to this question?" and drill down until you arrive at a Stage 1 question. The latter method requires multiple iterations as each stage is answered, whereas the former will typically lead to one path. Both provide opportunity for creative response.

If you're like me, your head hurts a little thinking about The Pickle. As a creative, you are accustomed to solving problems but less accustomed to designing them. However, growing stronger creatively requires a healthy understanding of problem design to create the richest environment for creative opportunity. When ideas are scarce, the vacuum is almost always caused by poor problem design. Alter the problem slightly, and you'll realize ideas in greater quantity and quality.

THE PICKLE IN PRACTICE

Let's run the three specific problems presented earlier through The Pickle to see where they fall and what the other stages may look like:

Stage 1: *I'd like bigger cabinets in the kitchen.*
Stage 2: *How can I get more kitchen storage?*
Stage 3: *How can I access kitchenware more conveniently?*
Stage 4: *How can I make cooking easier?*

Stage 1: *We need a brochure for our new product.*
Stage 2: *How do we tell more people about our new product?*
Stage 3: *How can we reach the most potential customers?*
Stage 4: *How do people consume media?*

Stage 1: *What kind of banner ads will get the most clicks?*
Stage 2: *What kind of online media is right for our audience?*
Stage 3: *Where should we advertise?*
Stage 4: *How can we increase profitability?*

In each case, the original question was a Stage 1 problem, but the other stages provide opportunity for creative solutions. In problem 1, bigger cabinets may be the right solution, but it seems like ideas that would solve Stage 3 have an opportunity to be more novel and more relevant. In problem 2, it doesn't appear that a brochure would have the most impact. Solving Stage 2 or 3 may produce more effective results. In problem 3, you may have to go all the way back to Stage 4 to ensure that dollars really should be spent on advertising. Perhaps a product alteration or a new distribution channel may serve profitability better. If advertising is the need, Stage 3 opens the door to many mediums and a host of creative solutions.

THE WRAP

Once you've placed the problem properly in The Pickle and you've filled out the other stages, you can begin developing ideas to solve the right problem. As you begin to immerse yourself in that problem, you'll often find that the solutions are still broadly defined. The "I don't know where this is going, but what if we…" scenario is common at this stage. This is a valuable part of the process, so don't avoid it. These are the germs of ideas that are needed to grow something creative. But these idea seeds need watering; they are complex organisms that often need to be separated and solved in pieces, and then brought back together as a creative whole. In the next chapter, you'll explore the process of solving the pieces.

SOLVING THE PIECES

You've been diving into the nuance of problem solving and with good cause. You can't be creative without problems to solve. However, the prickly aspect of problems is that they are rarely simple. Most problems are complex webs of cause and effect. If you solve one part well, another rises to whack you on the back of the leg with a stick. To effectively solve complex problems, you can benefit from breaking the problem into discernible mini-problems and then solving the pieces.

Problem dissection can present creative opportunities that could otherwise be missed if a problem is solved as a whole. Every problem can be dissected to reveal the unique challenges inherent in the resulting divisions. Like a business with designated departments, each department, although part of the whole, is its own entity with its own characteristics. Treating problems in the same way can help you discover prospects for creative solutions.

DISSECTING THE PROBLEM

In the IDEO shopping cart example in the "Introduction" of this book, the teams decided that the problem was too large to solve as a whole, so they split the project into four parts: shopping, safety, way finding, and checkout. The goal was to solve the pieces and then reassemble the solutions to achieve a stronger whole. This method strengthens relevance as smaller problems that may be overlooked by solving the larger problem. This is a regular function of the IDEO creative process and should be a regular part of yours as well.

The concept of problem dissection isn't difficult to understand, but that doesn't mean it's easy to accomplish. Like The Pickle, problem dissection is most effective when thought is given to proper categorization. The good news is that problem dissection fits well into the creative process that is explored in the *Creative Boot Camp* program. You fill out the stages of The Pickle and then choose the stage that offers the problem with the greatest opportunity for relevance and novelty. If that problem is still too complex to solve simply, you dissect the problem like you did that frog in fifth grade and solve the pieces.

SOLVING THE PIECES WITH DEWEY FINN

In an effort to illustrate how you might divide a problem and solve the pieces, let's use a hypothetical situation and break it down. Let's say your name is Dewey Finn and you're a jobless, wannabe rock star who is late on your rent. To earn some quick cash, you masquerade as your substitute, grade-school teacher roommate and take a temp gig teaching at a prep school.

In fact, this hypothetical situation isn't so hypothetical after all. This scenario is the setup to Paramount Pictures' 2003 musical comedy *The School of Rock*, starring Jack Black as Dewey Finn. In it, Dewey teaches a prep school class how to rock in an attempt to win a Battle of the Bands competition, restore his name, earn some money, and avoid discovery. After putting himself in the awkward situation of impersonating his roommate and accepting an invitation to fill in at the Horace Green Prep School without any real teaching qualifications, Dewey is presented with a problem—one that he solves through problem dissection. The problem: How can Dewey and the students prepare to win the Battle of the Bands without getting caught by Principal Mullins?

It's a big problem but one that has creative possibilities. Let's plug it in to The Pickle and see what the other stages produce.

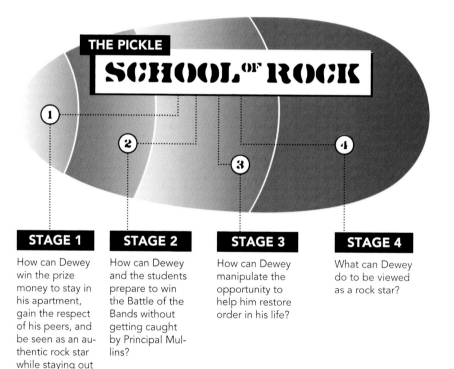

THE PICKLE

SCHOOL OF ROCK

STAGE 1	STAGE 2	STAGE 3	STAGE 4
How can Dewey win the prize money to stay in his apartment, gain the respect of his peers, and be seen as an authentic rock star while staying out of trouble and avoiding all the authority figures in his life?	How can Dewey and the students prepare to win the Battle of the Bands without getting caught by Principal Mullins?	How can Dewey manipulate the opportunity to help him restore order in his life?	What can Dewey do to be viewed as a rock star?

After reviewing the School of Rock Pickle, clearly, Stage 2 is the right problem for Dewey to solve. But to do so effectively, he needs to dissect the problem, divide it into pieces that can be solved individually, and then merge the pieces back together to (hopefully) solve the whole. Dewey divided his problem into four parts by identifying the obstacles that would inhibit him from producing a killer rock show:

The Band. To win the Battle of the Bands, he has to have real musicians. He stumbles on his class playing in the orchestra and believes that with a little training, he can mold them into an ample backup band to his lead guitar and vocals. He solves this problem by handpicking band members based on their instrument and talent. He spends most of his time training the musicians to not only play, but rock.

Security. If he is going to lead covert band practices instead of teaching from the curriculum, he needs a team of security personnel who can handle the smuggling of instruments in and out of the classroom, soundproofing the room, and ensuring safe and unnoticed passage to and from the parking lot during the tryout road trip.

Technology. In a modern-day rock show, technology plays a huge role in the overall experience. From synchronized lighting patterns to projection graphics, Dewey needs a savvy team of computer wizards to make the show a spectacle. He also needs the team to work with security to ensure that the hall-roaming principal is detected early so the ruse of a real classroom can be reset. Video cameras send the feed of hallway activity to the classroom computer, and recordings of Dewey teaching class help the tech team keep the charade alive while it monitors Principal Mullins' activity outside the classroom.

Marketing. Marketing is needed, not in the traditional sense of selling albums, but in the branding sense of selling an image. Dewey appoints a band manager and groupies, tasking them with management, costume design, naming the band, developing the logo, and creating merchandise. Dewey knows winning the Battle of the Bands means looking the part as much as sounding the part. The marketing team doesn't disappoint, naming the band The School of Rock and decking out each member in prep-school-inspired rock attire.

After solving each of the four pieces, Dewey brings the solutions together to solve the problem. They create the show, rock a legendary performance, and *almost* win the Battle of the Bands. Dewey pulls off weeks of undetected preparation, the students grow musically and relationally, and Dewey ends up starting a home business called The School of Rock with his roommate.

GETTING TO THE CORE OF THE PROBLEM

As with problem design, problem dissection relies on a strategic understanding of the varying facets of the problem. This means that as creatives, you must be willing to look beyond your execution medium of choice and get to the core of the problem. Whether you develop websites, write ads, design collateral, shoot videos, or build systems, strategic involvement must be part of your creative process if you intend on growing creatively. To do this, identify the restrictions that need to be overcome, grouping common obstacles together. Then take each of these groupings and summarize them in the form of a problem to solve. Dewey saw four significant obstacles he needed to overcome to produce his show: forming and training the band, providing security, using technology, and marketing the band. Let's look at another example of problem dissection in the form of a strategic training project.

DISSECTING A TRAINING PROBLEM

In 2009, my agency was approached by a pharmaceutical company with an interesting request: apply your creative process to sales rep training. It makes sense: Advertising's intent is to influence behavior, a response that could have significant benefits in a training atmosphere. If sales reps could become more engaged in training rather than only participating in the bare minimum to survive, they could increase their profitability through product and audience knowledge, critical thinking, and sales technique.

As is common with problem solvers, we had already formed our own hypothesis as to what we needed to build before we immersed ourselves in the problem. It is a natural human response to problem solving and often leads to expected solutions because these instant answers are typically influenced by something you have personally experienced. As you get more adept at solving problems, these initial solutions will come quicker and become increasingly more innovative and applicable, which is the result of purpose and practice. (In the next chapter, you'll explore a powerful training method for strengthening this skill: improvisation.)

As we explored the current training materials, it seemed clear that the information was written too clinically. It was difficult to apply. Our initial solution was to rewrite the training materials to be more conversational and include more application examples.

As it turned out, this solution was appropriate but shortsighted. After researching who was using these materials and how they were using them, we discovered that translation and applicability were only part of the problem. The sales reps were actively participating in the current training, but they were simply memorizing the information offered. None of it was sinking in. When a doctor asked them a question about the product, they would respond with canned phrases and marketing speak. They weren't able to critically analyze the question and form responses from actual understanding. This was prohibiting them from creating real relationships with their customers, a death knell in the pharmaceutical sales business. The training needed to promote critical analysis, not rogue memorization.

The problem was clearly bigger than we initially thought, so we ran the problem through The Pickle to ensure we were solving the right stage.

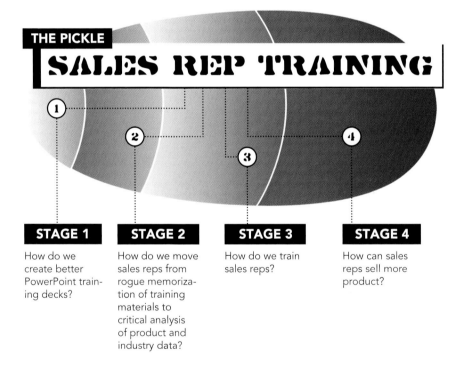

THE PICKLE

SALES REP TRAINING

STAGE 1

How do we create better PowerPoint training decks?

STAGE 2

How do we move sales reps from rogue memorization of training materials to critical analysis of product and industry data?

STAGE 3

How do we train sales reps?

STAGE 4

How can sales reps sell more product?

The exercise proved that we had the right problem, but we needed to solve this problem to a deeper degree to be effective. We dissected the problem by identifying the obstacles and started solving the pieces. Before we even knew what training medium we would use, we broke down the problem into three parts: learning design, environment, and tone.

Learning Design

When we began, we made the assumption that learning was a universal act, that age wasn't a factor in the process. What we discovered through our immersion into this problem was something else entirely: Adults exhibit specific learning behaviors that can be used to strengthen the effectiveness of training. Adults are task-oriented; they learn only as much as they need to accomplish the task at hand. Adults are also more resolved to learn in their preferred style; some are visual learners, whereas others covet voice-over. Some adults respond best to a physical instructor; others would rather study the written word in solitude. Additionally, adults have a great need to know their progress and comparative position to others on the same track: They have an innate desire to know how they are performing throughout the training exercise, how they compare to their colleagues, and what is expected of them.

The vast characteristics of our audience, along with the need to add content regularly, led us to choose a digital solution as the medium. We decided to build a website that would present content in a variety of ways—video, audio, and text—and provide downloads. The reps could choose the format that best suited them for every class on the site. They would be given regular progress quizzes and subject tests, and even summaries of their collective progress in the form of a score that they could compare with other reps. Solving this piece creatively helped lay the foundation for the other problem pieces.

Environment

Once a digital space was decided on, the varied technology consumption methods became a problem we needed to solve. The company issued standardized laptops to the reps, but we found that there was a vast array of devices that the reps used to manage their business. Technology adoption was all over the map; some reps were digitally savvy, whereas others were analog prone. How they interacted with the site would play as much of a factor in its success as the content they absorbed.

Our solution was to build a site that functioned on their company-issued laptop as well as any tablet they chose to use. We even built a mobile version of the site for those traveling reps who lived on their smartphones. In addition, we created a download function that would download the entire site content into a single formatted PDF file that they could print if they preferred a less digital experience.

Tone

Our research discovered that the tone of the content they were currently absorbing was academic and dull, which made it difficult to learn. We also discovered that their existing training process was riddled with learning obstructions. Reps would attend weekend training sessions that were administered by a host of experts, each developing their own visuals, methods, and expectations. Nothing felt consistent, from the design of the presentations to the tone of the content.

We employed our original idea of translation and applicability to the content, making it more conversational and human. Along with the improved content design, we developed a university analogy for the site and created a nomenclature and language based on buildings, subjects, classes, quizzes, and exams. The design of the site was consistent with the corporate brand but retained a contemporary look and feel. We even built a student lounge, a place where reps could come and socialize with other reps from all over the nation. If our intention was to encourage time on the site, we needed to make it a place where they wanted to hang out.

The Results

By solving these dissected problems, we were able to solve the greater problem of inciting critical analysis and understanding. Test scores skyrocketed, content was added regularly, and business increased dramatically over the first year the training site was live. Since that time, the site has grown to provide daily video updates from regional team leaders, rep customizations of interface elements, and incentive programs for class, subject, building, and yearly accomplishments.

THE WRAP

Problem dissection is vital to creative growth, but it is only part of the *Creative Boot Camp* program. It is true that a well-defined problem will inspire ideas in greater quantity and quality, as does the ability to recognize the obstacles to a solution, segregate those obstacles, and solve them individually. But equally beneficial to the work it takes to grow is something we often see as the opposite of work.

Physical trainers will say that to reach peak physical condition, you have to fool the body on a regular basis because the body adapts to exercise. If you do the same exercise regularly, you will see tapering results as your bodies get accustomed to the exercise and compensate. You have to change how you train to keep your body guessing by finding exercises that work the same muscles in different ways.

Creative training is very similar. The creative mind becomes accustomed to solving problems in similar ways; you develop a routine as a response to millions of tiny decisions you have to make on a daily basis. You solve problems at such a resounding pace that you have to purposefully change your tactic to reach optimal creative levels. In the next chapter, you'll discover that this requires finding methods to practice problem solving in different ways by removing consequence, creating a positive mind-set, and turning off your inner critic. In other words, you have to play.

PLAY IS THE NEW WORK

Three conditions for creativity need to exist: purpose, restriction, and action. You can have purpose and restriction, but if there is no action, you cannot be creative. That is where play comes in. Play delivers action.

Play and creativity share many common characteristics, the least of which is the lessening of consequence. The fear of consequence inhibits your ability to risk, and without risk, novelty is dead on arrival. Play can help circumvent consequence and train you to be fearless in your ideation.

A KATALYST FOR CREATIVITY

Kevin Carroll was working for the Philadelphia 76ers in 1997 when Nike asked him to join its company. The company was looking to fill a specific position; instead, the powers that be felt they had to bring his unique experiences as an athlete, trainer, and play advocate into the fold. Kevin's role was defined by his title, Creative Katalyst (K for Kevin, of course), and he immediately built a creativity center on the Nike campus where anyone at Nike could visit and immerse themselves in any number of creative activities.

One morning he peered out of his office window to see the steady stream of Nike employees walking from the parking lot to their associated buildings. Flabbergasted, he noticed how slowly they walked, and how they appeared to be dreading the day ahead. He thought, this is Nike—the most innovative, forward-thinking brand in the world! How can people dread working here? So he set out to remind them of how much fun working at Nike can be.

The next day he sent out a company-wide memo. For the rest of the week, the entire company would play a giant game of tag. He had a series of mesh jerseys emblazoned with IT across them—jerseys that he passed out randomly on the first day of the game. For the remainder of the week, if you were tagged by a person wearing an IT jersey, you were IT.

Throughout the rest of the week, Kevin periodically witnessed the result of his playful diversion. Secretaries ran across common areas of the Nike campus with their arms flailing and wildly laughing as they were chased by account salesmen in shirts and ties with mesh IT jerseys pulled down over them. Photos on bulletin boards highlighted those who were IT at some point during the week, and warning emails of the currently known ITs at any particular moment made the rounds. In just a few days, a simple game of tag had transformed the mind-set of thousands of people.

So popular was the experience that Nike created a TV spot around the idea that featured a young man in a major metropolitan area being tagged on the shoulder as IT. He then runs through the streets trying to tag anyone in his reach but perpetually comes up short and must change course to rid himself of this playful identity.

Currently, Kevin Carroll is self-employed and travels the world as a Katalyst, committed to elevating the power of sport and play in people's lives. In his book, *The Red Rubber Ball at Work* (McGraw-Hill, 2008), Kevin details the relationship between play and work.

> *"Think back to your childhood and to the years dominated by playtime, when there were endless hours to fill and the only agenda was to be captivated in the moment, to have fun. Playtime was also productive time, even if as kids we did not realize it. What we thought was entertaining was also instructive. Activities we called soccer, tap dancing, marbles, double-dutch, blocks, and tag were also exercises in resourcefulness, planning, strategy, design, decision making, creativity, and risk taking."*

COMMONALITIES OF PLAY AND CREATIVITY

Play and creativity share a common set of characteristics. Both support a positive mind-set, both are driven toward a purpose, both need restrictions to thrive, and both minimize consequence. Play provides the optimal training environment for creativity because the very characteristics you need to be creative you express through play.

WHY YOU PLAY GAMES

Imagine you are playing a game. Games are meant to be fun; they provide entertainment. If they are not entertaining, you will not play. In a 2004 study on why people play games, player experience research firm XEODesign discovered four reasons why people play games:

- Hard fun (meaningful challenges)
- Easy fun (curiosity piqued and fulfilled)
- Altered states (fantasy or escape)
- People factor (social engagement)

Regardless of why you play games, your goal is the same: to win. But winning isn't always about beating the game or the other competitors. Winning takes many forms that are intrinsic and extrinsic. Although the goal within play varies, what turns an activity into a game are the rules that are in place to which everyone playing agrees to adhere. You need rules to set a structure that guides play and leads you toward the goal. Games provide an atmosphere of lessened consequence. The risk/reward ratio of a game is what dictates the fun quotient.

PLAY AS BRAINSTORMING

Now, imagine that you and some of your coworkers are in a brainstorming session, which is limited to 75 minutes. Paper is spread out across the table, and it is littered with markers, crayons, Play-Doh, pipe cleaners, paper clips, and clothespins. You start the session with a warm-up exercise: build a make-shift mousetrap in three minutes. You then begin sharing ideas that will solve the problem. The problem provides a meaningful challenge, the shared ideas initiate a wealth of new ideas, the time feels like a reprieve from the mundane tasks you were performing prior to the brainstorming session, and the people you're with are open, accepting, and trustworthy. The goal of the session is clear: quantity. The ideas flow freely as you recognize that the group has only 15 minutes left in the brainstorming session. All ideas are written on the paper tablecloth and no one can judge an idea. It doesn't matter what ideas are shared; they are all valid during this time. You are not solving the problem during this time; you are simply offering options. It is impossible to be wrong.

CREATIVE TRAINING AND STRATEGIC PLAY

If creativity is a skill that can be trained, you can use play to train creativity. In the same way a physical trainer will mix up exercises to build the same muscle groups, you can insert play into the creative process and continue to train yourself to generate ideas in greater quantity and quality.

The key is to structure play strategically. People often perceive play as frivolous when in fact it can be strategic if the goal of play mirrors the goal of the problem you are solving. The first step is to recognize whether you are seeking one answer or multiple solutions.

CONVERGENT AND DIVERGENT THINKING

At the beginning of this book, I mentioned that I would not spend much time exploring the nuance of convergent and divergent thinking because dozens of other books communicate that concept in greater depth. However, it is helpful to have a basic understanding of the difference between the two. Doing so will help you see how and where play matters within the creative process.

Briefly, *convergent thinking* involves finding a singular answer to a problem. *Duncker's Candle Problem* in Chapter 2 was an example of convergent thinking. In that example, Duncker was researching a participant's ability to think creatively to solve a problem in the manner he had designed. He was looking for one answer, but it required creative problem solving to reach that conclusion.

Divergent thinking is the practice of generating as many possible solutions as possible. For example, if I asked you to write down as many uses for a paper clip as you can, you would be using divergent thinking. Divergent thinking is *quantity*; convergent thinking is *quality*.

Strategic play is the practice of forming convergent and divergent thinking into playful activity. If the goal of the problem you are trying to solve is to arrive at the one right answer, playful activities that encourage convergent thinking is strategic play. If the goal is to arrive at many possible solutions, games that encourage divergent thinking is strategic play. Creative training teaches you how to move back and forth between the two.

Tim Brown, CEO of IDEO, puts it this way:

> *"The first thing to remember is that play is not anarchy. Play has rules, especially when it's group play. When kids play tea party, or they play cops and robbers, they're following a script that they've agreed to. And it's this code negotiation that leads to productive play. But there aren't just rules about how to play; there are rules about when to play. Kids don't play all the time, obviously. They transition in and out of it, and good teachers spend a lot of time thinking about how to move kids through these experiences. As designers, we need to be able to transition in and out of play also.*
>
> *I think what's very different about design is that we go through these two very distinctive modes of operation. We go through a sort of generative mode, where we're exploring many ideas; and then we come back together*

*again, and come back looking for that solution, and
developing that solution. I think they're two quite different
modes: divergence and convergence. And I think it's
probably in the divergent mode that we most need
playfulness. Perhaps in convergent mode we need to be
more serious. And so being able to move between those
modes is really quite important. Because it's very easy
to fall into the trap that these states are absolute. You're
either playful or you're serious, and you can't be both.
But that's not really true: you can be a serious professional
adult and, at times, be playful. It's not an either/or; it's an
'and.' You can be serious and play."*

FRAMING THE PROBLEM BY MIRRORING THE PROCESS

A common practice I use when leading brainstorming sessions is to
reframe the core of the problem as something playful. By mirroring
the problem, the participants are practicing the very skills needed
to solve the problem while minimizing the consequence of reality.
You can think of it like taking practice swings while playing golf.
You stand behind the ball and take practice swings in a similar
environment to gauge what you need to do when you formally
address the ball.

For instance, let's say the problem is to generate ideas for an online
ad campaign for a pharmaceutical client. The FDA regulations
provide ample restrictions and often lead to less-than creative
results. Generating ideas to circumvent those rules is difficult, so
beginning with a playful exercise that mirrors that scenario practices
the same process without adding the same consequence.

Perhaps start with an exercise that asks participants to draw pictures
representing words without drawing the item described by the word.
Let's say the words were dog, gun, and clock. Participants would

be asked to draw pictures that lead someone to guess the identity of those three things without drawing a dog, gun, or clock. This is a playful practice that mirrors the actual problem of circumventing FDA restrictions: generate ideas for an online ad campaign about a pharmaceutical product without showing the product, giving its name, or declaring what it does.

IMPROVISATION AND CREATIVITY

Along with play, another entity shares many of the same characteristics as creativity. It's called *improv*. It can be defined as play, but it can also be defined as art. It mirrors creativity so strongly that even short exposures to it have significant results. Think of it as an extreme workout program for creative training. Extreme fitness programs are world renowned for their intensity and quick results. Improv is creativity's extreme training program as well.

Improv, or improvisational theater, is a performance art that requires actors to perform without a script and react to other actors, their surroundings, the audience, or predefined performance rules. As a source of inspiration, improv actors frequently solicit ideas for skits from an audience, building scenes and relationships from the suggestions. Most improv is meant to be comedic, but there are forms of non-comedic improv that utilize the same general structure of reaction.

You might recall that short-form improv was used in the popular late 90s TV comedy *Whose Line Is It Anyway?* hosted by Drew Carey. Improvisers would take suggestions from the audience or play improv games in a game show format. The group would be given scenarios, such as *you're at an airport ticket counter trying to get on a plane.* Then the host would apply the restrictions; for instance, *this performer will start the conversation with the letter M. Each performer can only use a single sentence, and that sentence has to begin with the next letter of the alphabet.* The on-the-spot nature of the skits and the quick-witted comedic strength of the actors created the appeal.

SIMILARITIES BETWEEN PLAY AND IMPROV

As with play, improv encourages a positive mind-set, is driven toward a purpose, needs restrictions, and thrives when consequences are minimized. However, improv also trains participants to make bold choices and to shut down their inner critic—both nourishing skills in creative growth. Improvisers have been trained, consciously or unconsciously, to be experts in creative thinking.

Nathan Stewart has been an improviser for 16 years, performing with the Kansas City, Missouri-based improv group Babelfish. He also has an undergraduate degree in International Business and an MBA in Marketing. He works for InTouch Solutions, a massive digitally focused creative agency that serves the pharmaceuticals industry. It's safe to say that Stewart knows a thing or two about the practical connections between creativity and improv. As a Senior Search Analyst in a creative agency by day and an improviser by night, he has experienced how each has trained him for the other:

> *"Improv teaches you to truly understand what we need to communicate in its simplest form, and that skill is exactly what we use when we generate ideas for our clients. Improv requires that we be open to things we can't control and to deal with them. In improv, if a player takes the scene in a direction I wasn't expecting, which is nearly every time, I can't stop to ask why, I have to be open to this new direction and just go. Improv is learning how to generate ideas and not filter them, it's a process that asks and rewards little braveries. It's collective brainstorming;*

the only difference is that in improv, we generate an idea then build on it rather than generating multiple ideas. We build vertically, and that gets to what works really quickly."

TRAINING TECHNIQUES FOR IMPROV

Training techniques for improv differ depending on the experience of the players, but a common training exercise for beginners is called *Yes And*. The exercise requires two people to engage in a conversation that begins with some form of outside inspiration. One player provides an initial sentence, and the two players then must build on that sentence by starting each sentence with "Yes, and…" and then completing their contribution. Starting every sentence with "Yes, and…" forces players to accept whatever reality is currently on the table and build on it. There is no stopping to say, "That doesn't make sense" or "What am I supposed to say to that?" Players must accept what was offered and build on it.

Many improv training sessions involve improv games that are meant to practice unscripted response and provide entertainment. A game called Old Job, New Job gives two players a job title. As they improvise doing that job, they are given the job title they had in a previous life. The players then start to mix characteristics of their previous job into their current job. Hilarity ensues when tax preparers begin to mix in the common actions of a butcher et al.

The format of these short-form games provides the comedic structure; all the players have to do is act them out truthfully.

The game Evil Stick of Gum requires players to improvise a scene given to them by the audience. But one of the players is chewing an evil stick of gum that can speak. The goal of the gum is to get the chewer in trouble. The other people in the scene don't know the actor is chewing an evil stick of gum, so they naturally think the words are coming from the chewer. You can see where the natural comedy lies.

ELIMINATING CONSEQUENCES

Acceptance of failure is an inherent characteristic of improv and one that serves creative growth as well. When players are engaged in a scene, they have to completely suspend the fear of consequence. Stewart says, "Once I'm on, I have no thought of consequence. I'm just trying to be true and trust the other guys on stage to pick me up. I don't have time to consider consequence, and even if I did, it wouldn't help. The result is better when the moment is simply honest. Honesty is better than evaluation, and we go to places that are more interesting if we don't worry about how we get there." This perspective plays equally well creatively. In a brainstorming session, removing consequence opens possibility, empowers creative problem solving, and puts more ideas on the table.

Like play, improv encourages action because that action is meant to be fun. When consequences are minimized, you are more willing to take part. "Improv is tissue paper," says Stewart. "It's very temporary; it's here then it's gone. There's no script; we have no idea where it is going to go, and that's why it is so appealing to audiences. They were part of something that only existed in that moment and will never be seen again. We have to *just go*. Strategy is important, but nothing is more important than *just go*."

COURAGE, CONFIDENCE, CREATIVITY

Improv is a powerful creative trainer and one that you will experience firsthand in the Creative Boot Camp program. There are a few limitations to improv that make it impractical to include in bulk, namely the need to practice with groups. But there are techniques and lessons that you can use within the program to train certain characteristics, the least of which is boldness.

Creativity, by its nature, is a call to remove yourself from your routine to see the world around you with fresh eyes. Kevin Carroll calls this perspective "having eyes like a child" because everything a child sees is for the first time. If you can teach yourself to see like a child, suspend your routine, and destroy your comfort zones, you'll find ideas everywhere. It takes courage and confidence to step out and just go. Stewart says it even takes confidence to play: "So much of what we do as improvisers and creatives is confidence; as an adult it takes confidence to play. Confidence in being OK with failure; that the consequences aren't greater than what you can achieve; and confidence that no matter what I contribute, it is real."

THE WRAP

Although play may not seem difficult to integrate into your creative training program, there are forces working against you. Creating habits are difficult because obstacles emerge to return you to your former state. Change is difficult to instill because it requires you to alter behavior that was built over time. Quietly, walls form to preserve the status quo. In the next chapter, you'll learn about the seven major obstacles you will face in your pursuit of creative growth and how to overcome them.

OVERCOMING THE OBSTACLES

Instilling any positive habit in your life, like the techniques for creative growth, will almost certainly be met with resistance because you are instituting behavioral change. These changes require self-control, and research has shown that self-control is actually an exhaustible resource. You have only so much to give, so you often let those obstacles force you to slip back into your routine. Eventually, these slips lead to feelings of guilt, and to remove that guilt, you give up the fight.

The first step to overcoming those obstacles is to recognize them. This is harder than it seems. The reason the obstacles exist is because they are difficult to foresee. They seep into your routine quietly and take root. If you can recognize the symptoms of these viruses, you can prepare to overcome them.

JUMPING THE LINE

Troy Polamalu has played the safety position in the National Football League for more than a decade. As a defender, his job is to stop the ball from advancing. The most effective way to do that is to stop the ball carrier before he gets to the line of scrimmage. But a number of hefty offensive linemen try to block him from doing his job. The average size of a lineman in the NFL is 6'3" and upwards of 300 pounds, and at least five of them at a time are between Polamalu and the ball. That's almost a ton of obstacle hell-bent on keeping the 5'10", 200-pound defenseman from achieving his goal. Going through them is virtually impossible. Going around them is hit or miss. Going under them is, well, unadvised. That leaves only one choice.

Polamalu has the uncanny knack of timing the snap of the ball perfectly and hurling his body over the offensive line just as the ball reaches the quarterback. This move is a high-risk/high-reward type of play. If Polamalu is a nanosecond early, it is a penalty. If he is a nanosecond late, the linemen pick him up and he is defenseless. Timed perfectly, however, and he avoids the line while stopping the advance of the ball before it even gets started. It seems like a simple response to an obstacle: Weigh all of the options and choose the path of least resistance. But few in a position that view brute strength as the greatest asset are able to put aside decades of conventional wisdom and overcome obstacles with a new perspective. This is exactly what you need to do when the obstacles of creative growth arise.

You can take a couple of steps to reduce your backward slips, or at the very least, minimize the guilt you normally associate with them. The first is to understand what stage of change you are in, and the second is to understand what obstacles you will need to overcome.

IDENTIFYING THE STAGES OF CHANGE

In the 1980s, two researchers, James Prochaska and Carlo DiClemente, developed the Transtheoretical Model for Behavioral Change. This model presumes that at any given time, a person is in one of five stages of change: precontemplation, contemplation, preparation, action, or maintenance.

Right now, you are in the preparation stage of this model. The action stage will take place as soon as you start the exercise program. The maintenance stage will commence when you have completed the program and are trying to maintain creative growth on your own. Creative Boot Camp offers strategies for the last three stages: preparation, action, and maintenance. Recognizing the stage you are in helps determine your strategy moving forward and identifies the path ahead.

PINPOINTING THE SETBACKS

It is also imperative that you recognize the obstacles that will keep you from achieving your goals. You can't fight what you can't see. For example, if you are attempting to create the positive habit of healthy eating and you visit a friend who is having a surprise party that offers 14 different types of cupcakes, you will struggle to maintain your self-control. But if you know that obstacle is coming, you can prepare for it by eating a healthy meal beforehand and bringing nutritious snacks to gnaw on.

SEVEN OBSTACLES IN CREATIVE TRAINING

You will encounter seven major philosophical obstacles as you engage in creative training. You will find little opposition to some while you struggle to understand others. Simply recognizing that they exist and being prepared to combat them will ensure that your pursuit of creative growth stays on the right track.

1 Pushed Forward vs. Pulled Back

Think about the ideas that you typically generate. Perhaps they are ideas for an ad campaign, a logo design, a short story, a photo series, a cartoon strip, or any number of other ideas. Do those ideas need to be pushed forward a little (or a lot) to be great ideas? Most people generate average to above-average ideas because they are almost always based on ideas they have personally experienced. By that standard, the novelty of those ideas is lessened and they require a push to make them bigger ideas. Generating ideas based on personally experienced solutions is an obstacle that you rarely recognize but one that has a dramatic effect on the quality of the ideas you produce.

To overcome this obstacle, you should strive to generate ideas that have to be pulled back instead of pushed forward, ideas that are a bit too novel or too relevant and require some restraint. This leads you to consider solutions that you've never experienced or can personally execute. In 2012, Old Spice ad agency W+K Portland had an idea to take commercial star Terry Crews and film him making music by flexing his muscles. That idea was a "pushed forward" type of idea because the novelty quotient on the idea was low. But the agency turned it into a "pulled back" idea when it explored working with VFK company The Mill and streaming video giant Vimeo to see if it was possible to give viewers the ability to play various notes on Terry Crews's muscles with their keyboards—in the video. The idea never needed to be pulled back because their exploration led them to develop a new form of interactive video experience. But it highlights the type of ideation you should aim to produce.

② Input vs. Output

As a creative, you spend a majority of your professional life executing ideas. You spend little time generating ideas and even less time preparing to generate ideas. You are outputting machines, applying your talents and skills to seeing your ideas come to fruition. Much of the value others see in you and you see in yourself comes from your ability to output because it is the tangible result of your work. Even your titles are output related: designer, writer, photographer, and producer. It is rare to come across creatives who are given the title thinker, ideator, problem solver, or imaginator, even though that is the primary component of their work.

In the early days of computer science, programmers used to apply the term GIGO, or Garbage In, Garbage Out, to their work. This was a term used to describe nonsensical output from nonsensical input. If you feed a computer faulty information, it will return faulty conclusions. The same applies to creativity. You output what you input. When your ideas seem ordinary and expected, you can almost always find ordinary and expected input mechanisms. Creatives feed off of inspiration; you need to fill your creative wells on a regular basis with the things that inspire you. Whether it's movies, music, conversation, or experience, if it inspires you, you need it. Don't take input for granted; make time to fill the well and strengthen your output.

③ Artistic vs. Creative

It is common to hear someone say, "I'm not creative." You usually hear this after the person in question has butchered a drawing or produced a stick figure representation of some event. What the person really means to say is, "I'm not artistic." Society has merged the idea of creative and artistic together. Artistry is making beauty. Creativity is problem solving. If that person was drawing stick figures to communicate an event, the irony is that the individual was actually being creative. The person was solving a problem and using a stick figure representation to do it. Regardless of the quality of the illustration, if the idea was communicated, the individual was creative.

If you can determine without reservation that you are creative, then you can overcome the artistic quality obstacle that affects your confidence in communication. When you get hung up on your inability to execute ideas, it affects your ability to first generate ideas and then share them. In short, you develop only the ideas you can personally execute. Your hands become the gauge on the validity of the ideas you produce. When you limit ideation this way, you put a cap on growth. Viewing creativity as problem solving opens you up to an infinite space for creative triumphs.

4 Present vs. Aware

Everyone has a story of a meeting that they attended in which a question was asked of them and they were unprepared to respond. Not because they didn't know the answer but because they weren't paying attention to the question or the discussion that occurred before the question. They had zoned out, bored or distracted into a state of intellectual Jell-O. Were you *present* during the meeting? Absolutely. Were you *aware* during the meeting? Not so much. Unfortunately, you approach your everyday creative existence the same way, and you fail to realize it. You've made every day a routine, and that routine keeps you from seeing the creative possibilities that surround you.

You may be present in your creative space, but are you aware? There's a story about a famous designer who produced a wonderful poster design of a young woman made entirely of scribbles. When asked where she got the inspiration to use the scribbles as an illustration technique, the designer replied that she reached for a pen to start thumbnailing and exploring illustration styles, and accidentally knocked over her cup of pens. When she returned the cup, she noticed the scribbles that layered the bottom of the cup. The scribbles were made from years of open pens being knocked around inside the cup. Inspired, she used that technique to create the illustration. What inspiration is within your reach right now? Train yourself to be more aware of your surroundings by challenging yourself to use something you can see or find nearby in your work. Take a different way home from work every day this week. Take visual notes (drawing-based notes) in at least one meeting per week. Take purposeful steps to see your everyday in a new way, and creativity will follow.

5 Solution vs. Answer

You have been conditioned to believe that for every problem there is one answer. You memorize answers so that you can recall them when you are asked. When you do so quickly, you are rewarded. When you hesitate or produce anything other than the approved answer, you are not rewarded. You've been told this is what constitutes failure: the inability to produce the expected answer. Because failure is unacceptable in society, you produce answers even if you don't know why. Answers are singular, and there is plenty of need for answers. Math should have answers. Physics should have answers. Creativity should have solutions.

Solutions are not singular; they are plural because there are many. Solutions are derived from critical analysis, breaking down a problem to see the possibilities. Solutions have degrees. Some solve the problem better than others, but you'll never know until you test a solution to see. Creativity is not problem answering. Creativity is problem solving. It implies a process that is seminal to the discovery. If you want to grow creatively, you must pass on answers and work to provide solutions. There is no easy solution; all solutions are the result of exploration. Creativity is found in solutions, not answers.

6 Effort vs. Value

Creativity is an expense. It comes at the cost of time, energy, and emotion. Weighing creativity as a cost enables you to make conscious, strategic decisions regarding what problems are worth solving and what are worth saving. Some fights are worth fighting, and others are better left alone. All creatives have a common battle: apathy—not yours but those around you. Others simply don't care about the nuance of problem solving to the degree that you do. So before you draw your battle line at the size of the font or the color of the background, weigh the value.

With any creative effort, there is a fluctuating scale of value. Some creative solutions are small and have little significance to the larger problem. Others have merit and are worth fighting for. You must learn where your effort is best spent. That's not to say the size of the font or the color of the background isn't a worthy fight. The key is to weigh each fight before gearing up for war. Everyone has a finite amount of creative energy stored up. You store energy when you input, but like a gas tank, it will decrease every time you turn on the engine. You must be able to decide which battles are worth the cost and which you can overlook for the greater good. Without this conscious effort, you will continually run dry and the problems that truly deserve creative solutions will go unsolved.

(7) Inspiration vs. Motivation

Inspiration has historically been an elusive conceptual state—one that creatives constantly seek and often credit for their most spirited efforts and imaginative work. It has also been the convenient scapegoat for expected ideas and mailed-in executions. Creativity feeds off of inspiration, like a perpetual energy bar for enlightenment. The more habitual cause behind your most unremarkable solutions, however, isn't the lack of *inspiration* but the absence of *motivation*. The key to overcoming either is understanding the difference.

Inspiration is the process of being mentally stimulated to do something, especially something creative. It is derived from a Middle English term translated as "divine guidance." Motivation is the general desire of someone to do something. It, too, comes from a Middle English term, but its translation is "to move." The notable difference is that one is defined as an external force, and the other is defined as an internal drive. Inspiration has you waiting impatiently for something to happen *to* you, which you can do little about unless it chooses to impart brilliance upon you. Motivation, however, is in your control. It comes from within and propels you to *act*.

When you are evaluating your creative energy and output, do you confuse inspiration with motivation? Although still infinitely valuable, inspiration can be found anywhere: on any website, in any magazine, on every desk, and around every corner—if you're willing to look for it. Motivation to act on everyday inspiration, however, is the source of continuous fuel that could be the accelerant you need to produce ideas in greater quantity and quality.

THE WRAP

You'll encounter the aforementioned seven major hurdles on your creative growth journey, but this is not an exhaustive list. Each of you will have minor setbacks along the way. This is an inevitable part of behavioral change. But as described earlier, when you have these setbacks, guilt sets in, and it's how you respond to that guilt that will determine your success in the Creative Boot Camp program. You can give up and alleviate that guilt, or you can press through and refuse to allow setbacks to deter you from reaching your goals.

So how do you know that you are reaching your goals? Does creativity have benchmarks that you can see? How do you measure creativity? In the next chapter, you'll explore the measurements you will use to determine if you are indeed generating ideas in greater number and value.

MEASURING CREATIVITY

Measuring creativity is challenging at best. Few would even consider measuring something so abstract. But if creativity is problem solving and if it is a process that you can strengthen and grow with practice, then it isn't as abstract as you may think. Creativity can be measured, but any measurement mechanism is flawed from the start because a subjective human element cannot be removed from the equation: What is a good idea?

Although no empirical method to creative measurement has ever been formed, there have been studies conducted that have formed the basis of what we will use in Creative Boot Camp to measure the quantity and quality of your ideas.

CREATIVE CAPACITY AND SHARING IDEAS

Who are the most creative people you know? Think of them right now. Assuming you didn't answer "me," what makes them more creative than you? If you are able to answer that question, your response will fall into one of two camps: 1) the work they produce, or 2) the ideas they share. This is where you often mistake artistry for creativity. Are those people more creative than you, or are they simply more artistic than you? If you can say they are more creative, then camp #1 is irrelevant. The work they produce is of little consequence to their creative position. The only gauge that matters is the ideas they *share*, not the ideas they *produce*. You don't know the ideas they produce but *don't* share, so you can't use them to determine their creative capacity.

EXAMINING CREATIVITY TESTS

Researchers have developed a host of creativity-linked tests and exercises to attempt to measure creativity. Some tests focus on creative potential; other tests focus on artistic propensity. Some measure problem-solving capabilities at various age groups, whereas others are self-assessments of personality tendencies. Two significant studies emerged in the 60s and 70s that provided many of the baseline processes used for creative measurement.

In 1967, creative psychologist J.P. Guilford developed Guilford's Alternate Uses Task. In Chapter 6 I used an example of this test while exploring divergent thinking (an appropriate connection because it was Guilford who first identified the difference between convergent and divergent thinking). Guilford's Alternate Uses Task was an exercise in divergent thinking, testing participants on their ability to generate alternative uses for common household items like a paper clip. He then scored responses based on originality, fluency, flexibility, and elaboration.

The most widely used creativity test was built on Guilford's research. E. Paul Torrance developed the Torrance Tests of Creative Thinking (TTCT), which tested and studied not only divergent thinking but problem-solving skills as well. The tests' ease of administration and broad spectrum of data collected have made the TTCT the standard for creative testing.

However, neither of these measurement mechanisms is perfect. The human element of ideation is nearly impossible to measure empirically. What makes for a good idea is simply different to each person.

USING THE COMPARATIVE SCALING TECHNIQUE

Creative measurement will always be a flawed science. But that doesn't mean you can't measure creativity at all. You can employ a comparative scaling technique to gauge creative growth for your purposes within the Creative Boot Camp program. Like any creative measurement technique, it's not perfect, but it should provide you with a general assessment of creative progress.

Comparative scaling is the measurement of items without an absolute baseline; they are measured solely against one another. For example, it would be like asking, "Which of these two TVs has the better picture?" An absolute measurement would need to include every TV ever made, but that's simply not feasible. Even then, there is still the variable in what defines "best." By using comparative scaling, you can limit the variables and provide a foundation from which to measure growth. You don't need to measure what constitutes a creative solution, you need to measure what constituted a creative solution when you started and what constitutes a creative solution when you finish.

In the Creative Boot Camp program, you will use your two core creative goals as measurement guides: quantity and quality. Quantity is easier to measure with a degree of accuracy, but there are still human factors that prohibit the result from being undeniable fact. Quality has many factors that limit measurement accuracy, but you'll use comparative scaling to determine a closer measure.

ONLINE TRACKING IN THE CREATIVE BOOT CAMP PROGRAM

The Creative Boot Camp program is measured through an online program-tracking feature. You will be asked to create an account on the Creative Boot Camp website and periodically enter your exercise results. These results will be compared to your previous results and to the existing results of everyone else engaged in the program to determine a progress score. The scores are derived from a quantitative and qualitative analysis that determines where you are growth-wise throughout the program. Simply put, the site will combine the quantity and quality of ideas you produce within the tracking exercises and generate a progress score each week.

QUANTITY

The quantity of ideas is a simple metric that requires only the restriction of time to be measurable. You will be asked to complete a divergent thinking exercise in a specified time frame, and the number of responses you provide will constitute the quantity variable. You should have already participated in a similar exercise when you took the Pre-Test. Recall that you were asked to write down as many Medieval Times Happy Meal toys as you could in three minutes. As you engage in problem-solving exercises throughout the program and improve your creative strength, you will generate more ideas more often.

But quantity has a flaw: *Is any idea relevant?* It would be easy to generate more ideas for a problem if the ideas didn't need to be relevant. In the Pre-Test, you could write down MP3 player, spaceship, watch, or garage door opener, but those responses are inappropriate because they didn't exist in medieval times. The program assumes that the ideas you generate have an authentic significance and that your intention is to solve the problem at hand, not to "buck the system." For instance, if one of your responses to the Pre-Test was a watch and your intention was that it was a sundial attached to a leather strap, then that qualifies as relevant. The goal is to respond with authentic relevance in your intent.

Other human factors also come into play when quantity is measured. Obviously, the same exercise can't be administered twice; you would have preexisting solutions you could apply. Therefore, similar exercises must be administered—exercises that have similar characteristics and restrictions. Regardless of their similarities, no two questions will be precisely alike. One topic might inspire a multitude of responses, and another might be more abstract. Combine this with a host of human conditions, such as time of day, sleep, distractions, mind-set, and attitude, and you can see that even quantity can be affected.

QUALITY: NOVELTY AND RELEVANCE

Quality measurement provides even greater challenges. To accurately measure the quality of an idea, two characteristics are necessary: novelty and relevance. This is where you will employ a comparative scaling technique.

Novelty means "unique or different," but both have degrees. How unique? How different? For example, if you have an idea for an app and you search for other similar solutions and find five other apps that do what your app idea would do, is your idea still novel?

What if you find only one other app that fits the bill? Is your idea still unique? Even novelty has a human component that determines worth.

Relevance is an even more subjective measurement. What is a good idea? How do you determine whether an idea solved the problem well? Relevance is nearly impossible to measure with any statistical accuracy, so you'll use novelty as your qualitative guide. For each tracking exercise, you'll enter your solutions into the online tracking function. You will compare those responses to the most common responses to that exercise to determine the rarity of response. The more novel the response, the better score it will receive. Some conditions will be in place to offset the most inappropriate of those responses, but as discussed earlier, relevance is nearly impossible to measure accurately.

THE WRAP

I encourage you to simply do the best you can with what you have. Solve the problems with an intended authenticity, and you will see authentic growth. You will get out of the exercises what you put in. Creative measurement isn't perfect, and that's OK. *You* will be a much better judge of your creative growth than any score can dictate. There is no optimum plateau you need to reach to be "creative"; you already are. Like fitness training, all you have are the goals you set and the processes you create to reach those goals. Once you've reached those goals, you set new ones. Creative training is no different. Use the scoring system to set achievable goals, reach them, and then set new goals. This truly is a journey, not a destination.

The next chapter introduces you to the Creative Boot Camp program, how the program works, and what it entails. The action stage of the model for behavioral change is about to begin.

TRAINING PREP

Your 30-day Creative Boot Camp is about to begin. Take a moment to set aside 15 minutes each day for the next five weeks to participate in the program. Make some physical gesture to do this: put it on your digital calendar, write it in your physical calendar, alert the people or entities with influence over your calendar that this time is off-limits. Commit to 15 minutes of uninterrupted creative growth time each day, give yourself fully to the daily instruction, and you'll see results by the end of the program.

Each day presents a different challenge. Some of these challenges require writing or drawing, so have a notebook and writing utensil handy. Some challenges require digital photography, so ensure your smartphone is powered or you have access to a digital camera. Some challenges benefit from a partner, so identify a few people you can call upon to help you along the way. Most important, all of the challenges will require you to solve a problem in some way, so bring you're mental A-game each day. If you respond to the challenges and give an authentic effort, you will leave more creative than when you began.

EXERCISING YOUR CREATIVITY

Creative Boot Camp is a five-week program that features five focus sections, each lasting one week. Each section contains five exercises designed to be completed one per day. Each exercise describes the goal, provides a description, and explains the restrictions. No exercise will take more than 15 minutes to complete. The exercises are meant to be light and fun, so don't stress—enjoy them. Following each exercise is The Moral, a simple truth that will help you see the growth opportunity in each exercise.

The exercises span a variety of executional mediums: design, illustration, writing, photography, and improv. *Do not* get hung up on the quality of the execution. The result is irrelevant; the important element is the idea you produce. This is not Artist Boot Camp or Writers Boot Camp. The goal of Creative Boot Camp is to strengthen your problem-solving skills. It doesn't matter whether you are executing your ideas as words, pictures, photographs, or line drawings. Don't pass on exercises because you don't feel your executional skills are advanced enough. The program measures the quantity and quality of the ideas you generate, not your ability to write or draw.

Be open to new mediums, even if you struggle with completing the task. If you're a designer, don't be afraid to write. If you're a photographer, don't be afraid to draw. You will be exposed to some techniques that make you uncomfortable. Don't be discouraged or fearful; be confident and bold. Fight through the urge to skip the exercises that don't fall into your executional wheelhouse. If you truly want to generate ideas in greater quantity and quality, put aside pride and ego, and as Nathan Stewart put it, *"just go."*

You can complete the exercises on paper or onscreen. It is entirely up to you which you choose. It is helpful to keep a notebook of your solutions to use as a reference of the solutions you generated for later review. Most exercises are developed from real-life scenarios (although they may be extreme versions), so it is common for some solutions to be relevant for real-life work. Recording your solutions in a single notebook makes it easier to review them when the need arises.

COMPLETING SECTION PROGRESS EXERCISES

At the end of each week, you will be issued a section progress exercise. These divergent-thinking exercises must be completed within three minutes each. It is these time-restricted, section progress exercises that you will be tracking on the Creative Boot Camp website.

If you took the Pre-Test at the beginning of the book, you should have already registered at www.creativebootcamp.net and set up your account. It is free to register and track your progress. Along with the Pre-Test, you will enter your responses to each section progress exercise. After entering each, your Creative Boot Camp score will be updated and you will receive your new rank.

IMPROVING YOUR RANK

Every Creative Boot Camp participant starts off with the rank of Private. By completing each stage, you earn a promotion to a new rank and you recieve your new stripes:

Starting Rank: **Private**

Completion of Section 1: **Sergeant**

Completion of Section 2: **Lieutenant**

Completion of Section 3: **Captain**

Completion of Section 4: **Major**

Completion of Section 5: **Colonel**

Completion of Creative Boot Camp: **General**

To complete Creative Boot Camp and receive the rank of General, you must complete the Creative Boot Camp final exam. This is a divergent-thinking exam that will produce your final creative growth progress score.

TRACKING YOUR PROGRESS ONLINE

Although it is obviously not necessary, I encourage you to track your progress on the website. This provides a tangible metric and will give you the push and encouragement you need to stay the course and complete the program.

MORE TRAINING WITH OFFICER BOOSTER PACKS

After you have completed the program, you can then turn to the remaining chapters in the book. They detail steps you can take in the short term, midterm, and long term to ensure that your creative growth extends beyond the next five weeks. In addition, the website provides opportunities to continue the formal Creative Boot Camp training with Officer Booster Packs, which contain additional 30-day sets of exercises. You can track your progress on Officer Booster Packs on the website as well. The website also details opportunities to attend live, regional, Creative Boot Camp weekends.

FINDING AN ACCOUNTABILITY PARTNER

One last encouragement: consider finding an accountability partner for the program. The strongest way to ensure that you stick with the program is to do it with someone else. Your accountability partner doesn't even have to be in your physical environment. If you want to match up with an accountability partner online, check out the website for details.

TEN-HUT!

Ready, soldier? Put on your boots, fall in, and drop and give me 20 because Creative Boot Camp is on.

CHAPTER 9

STARTING FROM SCRATCH

You've all heard the phrase "starting from scratch." It's an old racing term that describes the removal of a handicap or head start. When all the racers started "from scratch," or from a literal line scratched in the turf, everyone started from the beginning.

When you're solving problems, how often do you start from scratch? In the Wieden + Kennedy office in London, the foyer features a mannequin with a blender for a head and a briefcase that says "WALK IN STUPID EVERY MORNING" written on the side. The strange sculpture is a reminder to throw aside the preexisting solutions of others and start from scratch every time a problem arises.

When you solve a problem, you typically begin with solutions others have devised. This is a normal, adult response to problem solving. So why reinvent the wheel if the solution works? The reason is that you'll never know if there is a better solution than the wheel if you don't put the wheel aside and rethink its purpose.

In this first week, you will be challenged to start from scratch, the genesis of creative thinking. Pay careful attention to the restrictions of the exercises you are given, and have fun. At the end of the week, you will complete a section progress exercise that will help gauge your progress through the program. Be sure to enter your responses into your training program guide at www.creativebootcamp.net.

1.1

ULTIMATE DESK

TIME LIMIT: 12 MINUTES

You know what the world needs? More desks! You've been sitting behind a desk of some form for almost your entire professional life. Well, it's time to chuck that 1974 metal monstrosity out your office window and come up with the kick-buttiest desk ever created by man, woman, or hermaphrodite.

You are charged with designing the ultimate desk. Fortunately, the venture capital wing of the federal government has commissioned you to design the perfect creative's desk. Money is no object; the department has money coming out the wazoo, so go nuts. Consider shape, function, power, the number of appropriate keg taps—whatever your twisted mind can conjure up. The only rule is that it has to actually perform the function of a desk in some way.

THE MORAL

When you began this Ultimate Desk exercise, where did you start? Most begin this exercise in the same way: They start with a desk. The question is why? The exercise never instructed you to start with a tabletop; it simply stated that "it has to actually perform the function of a desk in some way." Those that start with a desk imply that it must have a tabletop of some sort because the word used was "desk," and that word has a predefined meaning to everyone. In short, you placed restrictions on your ideas that weren't actually there.

I call this syndrome "attachism." We have become a society of attachers, trading true innovation for added improvement. You start with what you already know and then attach improvements. Very few people are able to remove themselves from what a desk is supposed to be to question how everyone currently uses a desk. What is the purpose of a desk now versus how we have transformed the historical version of a desk to fit our needs? To continue to grow creatively, you must train yourself to question every precedent and ensure that you are solving the right problem.

1.2

BUG'S RIDE

TIME LIMIT: 15 MINUTES

Bugs are, well, creepy. Most don't do any harm to humans, but there's just something about the feeling of probing tentacles walking slowly across your feet that cause even the bravest of creative to leap onto a chair and shriek like a banshee. But is it their fault that they're the size of, well, an ant? Bugs are actually a lot like people. They deserve to experience the thrill of speed and gravity without the fear of ending up squashed against someone's front bumper. And you're just the creative to give it to them!

Your task is to use whatever household junk, arts-and-crafts supplies, or any other needed building materials you can find in your immediate area to design a carnival ride for a bug. You can disassemble objects to use various parts, utilize your environment, or even find items to use as propellants if necessary. Think of yourself as a mini-Walt, and you're making Bugsneyland.

THE MORAL

Most solutions to Bug's Ride fall into one of four categories: coaster, slide, swing, or catapult. Although these may cover the gamut of most well-known carnival rides in existence today, it's the last category that is so compelling. Many solutions to this exercise involve some form of catapult that flings the bug across an expanse of space. My question to you is: What actual carnival ride does this?

The answer is none. Some do strap you to giant rubber bands and bounce you high in the air, but few propel you long distances, safety net or not. Yet, some creatives have no trouble building a catapult for a bug's carnival ride despite the inevitable outcome because they see bugs from their perspective only.

When Pixar animators started to do research for the movie *A Bug's Life*, they fixed a small camera onto a toy car and wheeled it around in the grass outside the corporate office to see what life looks like from a bug's perspective. When you generate ideas for your audiences, do you do the same?

BIG BOX HOME IMPROVEMENT BOUTIQUE

TIME LIMIT: 9 MINUTES

Traditionally, hardware store customer demographics have been largely male. Most big box, home-improvement meccas are designed for this demographic due to a cacophony of PVC pipes, wood smells, and power tools. The oldest operating hardware store in the United States has been selling to this portion of the population since 1782, offering over 200 years of man shopping and fix-it pedaling. It's time that the conventional hardware emporiums reach out to the ladies.

Your task today is to reimagine the common, big box hardware store for women. From the product offering to the design of the store, list the changes you would recommend to transform the typical hardware store from man center to lady complex. Anything and everything is negotiable.

THE MORAL

Stereotypes are often regarded as a combination of truth and exaggeration. You use stereotypes as an organizational method, a way of defining large groups of diverse people so you can better comprehend them. This is common when you address audiences in your creative work. You'll use terms like "target audience" and "intended market" to group consumers into buckets you can segregate and to which you can provide "individualized" messages. The great advantage of audience assumptions is that they are typically born from some form of truth, so if you can speak to that truth, you can reach that audience. The disadvantage of audience assumptions is that not all people adhere to the assumption.

As you completed this exercise, it was natural for you to stereotype women to find relatable, creative solutions. Stereotyping, despite the negative connotation, is not always negative. Some of these stereotypes are real, but some are not. As you generate ideas for your clients and for yourself, you should take the time to define what is true and what is false with the assumptions you make about your audiences so your ideas are met with attention, not apathy. Authenticity is required for an idea to be relevant.

EXPERT PROFESSOR

TIME LIMIT: 60 SECONDS

You are an expert at something. Be it a hobby, a sports team, an application, or a TV show, at least one topic could occupy significant time in a conversation. But it is probably safe to say that your knowledge on other subjects and objects is lacking. You might say you know absolutely nothing about a certain topic, but that wouldn't be true. Most likely, you could say something about that topic that would at least feign remedial knowledge for a short period of time. Let's test that theory today.

You can start this exercise in one of two ways: either with a partner or alone. If you have a partner, ask your partner to choose a random nearby item. If you are alone, open a book or magazine and randomly point to a word or object on a page. It can be a subject like the state budget, or it can be an object like a stapler. Choose your random subject or object, and keep it in your mind.

For the next 60 seconds, tell a story about that subject or object as if you are an expert in whatever it is. Avoid the urge to pause, and just keep talking. Keep your monologue going for the full 60 seconds; make up facts and anecdotes as you go along, and remember that body language matters! Be convincing, even if the words you are saying are complete rubbish.

THE MORAL

In this improv exercise, you demonstrated that you have a rudimentary knowledge of most subjects but rarely a complete knowledge of anything. If you wanted to become an expert in the subject or object that you just ranted about for 60 seconds, you would read about and research it, and you would break down the subject to understand the nuances or disassemble the object to learn about the parts. In short, you would learn.

Do you take that same approach when you are generating ideas for your clients or for yourself? Or do you rely on what you know and make up the rest? You can fake a decent knowledge base for just about any subject, but creativity requires you to delve deeper to find authentic truths below a surface-level understanding and bring those to the forefront. Like IDEO's shopping cart exercise, be willing to become an expert in the problem to find relevant solutions.

THE MAGICAL MYSTERY TOUR BUS

TIME LIMIT: 12 MINUTES

Rock stars tour the country in style, traveling in luxury apartments known as the tour bus. From Jacuzzis and saunas to animal cages and recording studios, these wheeled suites afford the rich and famous a rich and famous ride. Have you ever wondered what it would be like to have your own decked-out tour bus? It's time to give that fantasy some legs—or wheels, as it were.

Your task is to design the world's greatest tour bus. If you had an unlimited budget and were going to travel around the country for weeks at a time, what would your tour bus include? Create your ideal tour bus and let the road trips begin!

THE MORAL

If you applied The Pickle to this exercise, you could say that the problem you solved was entirely inside the tour bus. How luxurious did you make the inside of this rolling space that is the size and shape of a traditional tour bus? But if you went back one stage, you may have extended the problem to include the actual bus. Which stage did you solve?

Solving the larger problem isn't always in your control. But even if you are directed to solve the smaller problem, choosing to step back a stage and solve the larger problem can help identify new ideas within the smaller one. If your ideas for this exercise started with a tour bus that was the size of a car transport, you could include a much wider range of luxuries, like full swimming pools or roller coasters. You could use that freedom to help generate ideas for the greater restriction, say converting to endless pools with swimming machines made for smaller spaces or virtual roller coasters on tilting tracks. Generate ideas for the larger stage, and you may find inspired ideas for the smaller stages.

PROGRESS EXERCISE

Enter your solutions into the Section 1 Progress Exercise guide from your dashboard at www.creativebootcamp.net to keep track of your creative progress.

CRACKERJACKIMUS

TIME LIMIT: 3 MINUTES

In 1912, Cracker Jack started putting prize coupons in its popular boxes of caramel-coated popcorn and peanuts. Kids loved the treats but felt frustrated over the wait to get the mail-order prizes. So the owners of the company started to insert paper-wrapped prizes right into the box. This proved to be the winning combination as scores of snack-infused kids fell in love with the prizes as much as the munchies. But plenty of kids in other historical eras never got to enjoy the hunt for that snack-encased treasure—whatever that may have been in their time. Let's find out.

For your Section 1 progress exercise, you have 3 minutes to write down as many Cracker Jack toys as you can think of if Cracker Jack existed in ancient Rome. What would Romans have put in those boxes as prizes? Write down as many as you can; quantity is the goal. Good luck.

SECTION **1**

ROUNDUP

If there was a theme to this week, it would be hyperfocus. It is common to get so focused on the solution to a problem that it's easy to miss the forest for the trees. This occurs when you predefine the solution before understanding the entirety of the problem. When this happens, you fall back on what you know or think you know instead of what you learn. To grow creatively, you must be willing to pay careful attention to the problem that you are solving to ensure that it is the right problem and that the solutions you are generating are born from discovery, not precedent. This will help you to "walk in stupid every morning." Let's recap what you learned this week.

(1.1) ULTIMATE DESK: True innovation starts by evaluating the restrictions of a problem and identifying which restrictions are real and which are implied. You allow language and experience to mold an expected starting point for your ideas when you could be starting from scratch and generating novel solutions.

(1.2) BUG'S RIDE: For an idea to be relevant, it must be relevant to the audience that will consume it. It's easy to generate ideas that you find valuable, but you're not always the audience. To truly start from scratch, your focus should be on finding out how your audience sees the world so you can see where your ideas fit into their perspective.

(1.3) BIG BOX HOME IMPROVEMENT BOUTIQUE: When you generate ideas for your audience, not just for yourself, make sure you're not simply relying on what you think the audience finds valuable. Take the time to start from scratch, find what is authentic about the audience, and generate ideas to serve that attribute.

(1.4) EXPERT PROFESSOR: If you're like most people, you know a lot about a little and a little about a lot. This can hinder creativity because you rely on an incomplete initial picture of the problem as you set out to solve it. To grow creatively, you must first be willing to gain an in-depth understanding about the problems you solve before you intend to solve them.

(1.5) THE MAGICAL MYSTERY TOUR BUS: The creative process is just that, a process. Finding creative solutions takes effort. Sometimes, finding those nuggets of creativity require you to start from scratch to see the larger picture and solve the larger problems. Those insights can often lead to the most creative solutions.

Well done! Your first week is in the books. In Section 2, you'll find inspiration in your daily lives—inspiration you can use to solve problems with greater relevance and novelty.

SECTION 1

NUMBKILLER

Think back to a time when you felt inspired. Most likely, it was when you were enveloped by some type of expertise, whether it was when you were flipping through the pages of a design annual or walking the halls of a museum. You are inspired when you experience something you feel is beyond you—for example, an idea you don't think you could have generated or a work of art you don't believe you could have made. In Chapter 7, you discovered inspiration is a force you encounter. What if you could encounter it right at your desk?

One of the common traits shared by highly creative people is that they find inspiration in their everyday experiences. It could be a songwriter who writes of a simple moment he experienced or a photographer who finds the beauty of a shadow falling from a bottle of water. Your normal day is a bastion of inspiration if you learn to see it differently than you currently do. As you create routine in your lives, you create a habit of viewing things as the function they serve. This is a fundamental creative flaw of adulthood. Children have no problem seeing everyday objects as more than what they are. You see a pen cup, they see a spaceship. You've become numb to the possibilities that surround you in the very places you inhabit most.

In this second week, you'll be asked to see your everyday differently—to find the solutions sitting next to you. At the end of the week, complete the section progress exercise and enter your responses into your training program guide at www.creativebootcamp.net.

EVERYDAY MONSTER

TIME LIMIT: 15 MINUTES

In 1818, Mary Shelley wrote a book about a scientist who created a monster by molding together various parts of deceased people and adding a little lightning as the life spark. The monster was Frankenstein, and few know that the book was the result of a dream Shelley had after she and a few friends placed a bet on who could write the best horror story. I suppose she won. Today, you'll channel your inner Dr. Frankenstein.

Your task is to create your own monster from whatever is in your reach right now. You must assemble the best monster you can create from these items and these items alone. If you happen to be reading this in a supply closet, you just won the lottery. This monster will serve as your mascot for the week, so display it proudly. Let it remind you that your everyday can produce wonders if you'll see the opportunities.

THE MORAL

Isn't it amazing how much is actually within arm's length of you most of your day? I'm betting that you were able to find more than enough materials to create a monster but struggled with adhesion. This is normal; unless you happened to have a roll of tape nearby, you were probably limited to what you could affix to your monster. This is where creative problem solving comes in. Because a monster has no particular shape it must take, you could have used anything for most of the monster. But there were times when you wanted to create something specific, such as eyes, horns, teeth, or a tail. In these instances, you most likely had to get creative.

Think about how often this is the case in your daily life. You are able to solve 90 percent of a problem without incident, but that last 10 percent requires some creative problem solving. It's that ornate play costume for your child on which the wings won't stay straight or that social media campaign that plateaus just short of the goal. Getting past that last 10 percent often requires you to shift gears, to introduce something new to solve a new problem or alter a plan to boost it past the finish line. It's at these times that your creativity is most evident—when you are able to find solutions in your everyday that finish the job.

HIGH-KOO

TIME LIMIT: 9 MINUTES

During the 17th century, Japanese poets began to use
a form of poem known as Hokku. It took many shapes
but was derived from a standard set of structural rules.
You know this type of short-form poetry today as haiku.
Although haiku has many configurations, one of the
most popular is based on a 5-7-5 syllable structure. It is
a three-line poem in which the first line has five syllables,
the second line has seven syllables, and the last line has
five syllables. An example of a haiku would look like this:

> **Creative Boot Camp**
> **The greatest book on the shelf**
> **If it is alone.**

Look around you right now and choose a random item.
Your task is to write a haiku about how that item could be
used as a weapon. How deadly a weapon is up to you.

Happy haiku hunting.

THE MORAL

I could have just tasked you to write a haiku about any object, but the minimal restrictions wouldn't have led to anything of interest. Simply describing an object isn't nearly as intriguing as assigning an alternate purpose to an object. In this case, I chose weaponry as the alternate purpose, but every object you can see right now can have infinite uses if you are able to look past its typical function.

Dalton Ghetti (www.daltonmghetti.com) is a carpenter and a sculptor who uses a pencil in his art. This may not seem like a very creative tool until you discover that he doesn't use the pencil to make the art, he uses the pencil as the art. Dalton Ghetti carves the graphite tips on pencils into sculptures. From tiny mailboxes and boots to busts of Elvis Presley and even interlinking hearts, Ghetti never uses a magnifying glass, only a razor blade, a sewing needle, and a sculpting knife. His work is an amazing testament to the alternate possibility you can see in your everyday.

CAPTURE CAPTIONS

TIME LIMIT: 10 MINUTES

For this exercise, you will need a smartphone or digital camera. It is a two-part exercise that requires you to take a photo of a random object or person in your area. Take that picture now and display it where you can see it by either displaying it on your smartphone or digital camera preview screen or by printing out the photo.

While looking at the item in the photo, take the next 10 minutes and write down as many captions to that picture as you can without calling out the name of the actual person or object. You can reference the item without naming it or call it by another name. Imagine that this photo will be in tomorrow's newspaper along with an article that you can't read. All you can read is the caption that accompanies the photo, so be sure to provide an idea as to why this photo is significant to whatever story it accompanies.

THE MORAL

In 1973, a game show debuted called The $10,000 Pyramid. The rules of the game were simple: A celebrity was given a series of words or phrases and had to describe them without using the actual words or phrases. The contestant would have to guess what word or phrase the celebrity was describing. The game became more difficult when challenging categories needed to be described, such as "Things you would pay extra for" or "Things that are crushed." The celebrity had to solve problems creatively and quickly for the contestant to win.

Although you may never be on a 70s era game show (that's a good bet), there are plenty of times when you'll need to generate multiple ideas about a central topic. The expected ideas—the ones that come easy—are referred to as "low-hanging fruit." These are the ideas that everyone sees. The desire is to get past these ideas to what lies beneath. But to do that, you have to document the low-hanging fruit so you can make room in your creative minds for something deeper. This is part of a mature creative process. Document those easy ideas so that they don't have to claim residence in your memory. As a result, you can work on something new.

2.4

INSTANT STORYTELLER

TIME LIMIT: 2 MINUTES

Every object you can see in your immediate surroundings has a story. The story may be how it was made, how it came to be in the place it is now, or how it is used. That story may be dull and lifeless, or it may tell a history that few know. In 1998, director François Girard filmed a movie called *The Red Violin*, a film about a 300-year-old violin and the four stories of that violin's existence as it passed from one owner to another. To those owners and throughout history, that violin represented anger, betrayal, love, and sacrifice. Although the stapler on your desk probably doesn't have as deep a story as *The Red Violin*, it could with your help.

Close your eyes. Wait, don't do that until after you have read this (my bad.) When you are instructed to at the end of this exercise, close your eyes and rotate your head left and right. Then open your eyes and focus on a single object in your view. For the next two minutes, tell the fictional story of that object. It can be about how it was made, what experiences it had, or how it came to be in that place. Be sure to tell the story out loud so you can hear your own voice. Try to keep talking for the entire two minutes, adding more to that object's fictional story. You can close your eyes now.

THE MORAL

You tell stories every day. Story is the oldest and most compelling form of communication known to man. You tell stories to teach, to warn, and to explain. You use story for entertainment and instruction. Where you seem to stop telling stories is in your creative work.

Every client, every product, and every cause for which you generate ideas has a story. That story may not seem compelling at first, but interest is the burden of the storyteller. As you generate ideas, do you lose track of the story behind the problem or do you focus on what story that problem could tell? If you can frame the problem in the form of a story, you may uncover a catalyst for creative solutions.

PHOTOCLATURE

TIME LIMIT: 15 MINUTES

Kids are great at finding recognizable objects in strange places. They see animals in the shapes of clouds and faces in industrial design. Adults have a harder time seeing anything other than the primary object. So now you'll practice seeing through the eyes of a child.

You'll need a smartphone with a camera or a digital camera for this exercise. Your task is to spell your first name in photos—one letter at a time. The only restriction is that you can't take a picture of an actual letter; you must find shapes in your area (and beyond if you need to venture outside of your immediate area) that look like those letterforms. Some letter shapes are easy to find, like O, I, and T; others are more difficult to find, like W, K, and Q. Take one photo for each letter, and find them in order so you have consecutive photos that spell your name. If your name is Toi, you can thank me later.

THE MORAL

How far were you willing to go in this exercise? Did you "settle" for shapes that were somewhat letter-like, or did you hold out to find shapes that were exact fits to the letterform? Did you manipulate anything to be more letter-like? Did you venture outside of your area to complete the exercise? Strangely enough, these are all questions you could ask when you have to solve problems for your clients and yourself.

How far are you willing to go to solve a problem for your client? Are you willing to settle for solutions that are somewhat creative, or will you hold out for solutions that solve the problem relevantly and with novelty? Will you manipulate the problem to fit a solution you've already generated, one you really like for any number of reasons? Are you willing to venture outside of your comfort zones to solve this problem and dig deep into the problem to learn as much as you can before setting off to solve it? These are the questions you need to ask every time you aim to solve a problem creatively.

2.5

2

PROGRESS EXERCISE

Enter your solutions into the Section 2 Progress Exercise guide from your dashboard at www.creativebootcamp.net to keep track of your creative progress.

THE SWISS PIRATE'S ARMY KNIFE

TIME LIMIT: 3 MINUTES

A pirate's life is simple: pillage, plunder, avoid the authorities, drink, sail, repeat. But even with such a simple life, a pirate has needs. No, not those needs, tool needs. Like most people, pirates could use a handy Swiss Army knife. If you're not familiar with the Swiss Army knife, it is a utilitarian pocket tool that contains any number of useful tools—a knife, magnifying glass, screwdriver, fork, spoon, corkscrew, and bottle opener. Your task today is to reimagine that tool for pirates.

For your section progress exercise, you'll write down as many Swiss Army knife tools as you can conjure up. They don't all have to be flat and fit into the standard Swiss Army knife shape. You can stretch the laws of physics to include whichever tools you think a pirate would need to perform his daily pirate duties. Write down as many as you can in three minutes' time.

ROUNDUP

This week you explored the creative possibilities in your everyday. Everything you need to be creative is within your grasp regardless of your environment. Your ability to see past regular purpose can help you develop creative solutions to even the most challenging problems. Sometimes, these small shifts in normal produce the largest ideas. Let's recap what you learned this week.

2.1 **EVERYDAY MONSTER:** Creativity is often most evident when you have to change gears in the middle of a problem to finish it off. This is where your quick-thinking training can benefit you the most. Find creative solutions in your everyday for the small problems that arise in everyday tasks.

2.2 **HIGH-KOO:** Are you able to see the alternate possibilities in situations? A mature creative can see past the functional purpose of an object to discover something greater. Whether it's how to use a social media platform in a different way or how to write about a product without using its name, alternative purposes exist all around you, and many of them could provide just the creative solution you are looking for.

2.3 **CAPTURE CAPTIONS:** Part of your creative process should include documenting ideas, even the easy ideas that seem to be available to everyone, because even obvious ideas take up space in your creative consciousness. Once you document them, you can focus on the great ideas that hide behind the good ones.

2.4 **INSTANT STORYTELLER:** Story is a powerful medium, and it is underused as a creative tool. You can use story to initiate ideas, uncover hidden gems, or even act as the idea. As you generate ideas, remember that there is always a story waiting to be told.

2.5 **PHOTOCLATURE:** There are lengths that you are willing to go for each problem you solve. Those lengths differ based on condition: time, effort, cost, and value. In each case, you must ask what lengths you're willing to go to solve a problem creatively. These boundaries will become the restrictions you use to frame the solution.

Two weeks down and three weeks to go. How do you feel? You should start to feel like you're making some progress. In Section 3, you'll explore the role of relevance in ideation, practicing the skill of starting with truth and elevating the novelty within it.

SECTION 2

FLAVORS OF RELEVANCE

Creativity is defined as problem solving with novelty and relevance. Although novelty may be the fluctuating creative factor, relevance is the standard by which all solutions are measured. Novelty is useless if the problem isn't solved. However, relevance isn't a cut-and-dry characteristic.

Relevance comes in many flavors: absolute, comparative, and subjective, just to name a few. To solve problems creatively, it helps to recognize what is the bare minimum required to actually solve the problem. This establishes the baseline and can be done with a simple question: What is the minimum outcome? If you can answer what is the least that should happen once the problem is solved, you can then define what solutions will be relevant.

For instance, if the problem is how to get someone elected to office, the bare minimum would seem to be votes for your candidate. But in reality there are two minimum solutions to this problem: either get your guy elected or make sure the other guy doesn't get elected. The real minimum isn't positive votes; it's election. This is comparative relevance. On the other hand, if the problem is naming a business, the minimum solution is absolute: a business name. Anything more is a matter of novelty.

In this third week, you'll explore different types of relevance that have an effect on the creative quotient of ideas. At the conclusion of the week, complete the section progress exercise and enter your responses into your training program guide at www.creativebootcamp.net.

3.1

WHAT'S NEXT?

TIME LIMIT: 11 MINUTES

Story is a powerful communication medium. One of the by-products of story is the concept of implication. By setting up a scenario, a storyteller can imply future events simply by creating order. For example, I was walking through a hotel that had recently been renovated. At 6'8", I am exactly the height of a standard door frame. But the hotel didn't install standard door frames; instead, the installed door frames were 6'5" in height. As I was walking down the hall toward the door, I had no reason to pay attention to the size of the door frame.

So what happened next?

Exactly. I don't need to tell you what happened, because the story implies my impending encounter with the door frame. This is a skill you'll practice today when you generate as many one-sentence completions to the following scenario as you can:

1. A man found a digital voice recorder lying in the street.

2. The device had a note taped to it that read, press play, so he did.

3.

Finish this scenario with as many possible conclusions as you can conjure in 11 minutes. Your solutions should be one sentence maximum.

THE MORAL

To solve this problem with any relevance, there is a significant restriction in play: the place in the story. A history exists that can't be ignored to solve this problem. Any solution that doesn't involve a man pressing the play button on a mysterious digital voice recorder simply isn't relevant. If your third answer was, "The man ate a bologna sandwich and fell asleep on a bench," the solution lacks relevancy because it never addresses the history present in the problem. Does it provide an ending? Yes. Is that ending relevant? No. So the bare minimum relevancy on this problem isn't closure; it's conclusion.

When you are solving problems creatively, do you ignore history? Keep in mind that there are opportunities to learn how people interacted with this problem before, and these opportunities can help shape your relevancy. When IDEO was redesigning the shopping cart, the company researched how people had historically used shopping carts so the designers could contrast their ideas with how people currently use shopping carts. When you generate creative ideas, become aware of the history behind the problem. It can help shape the solution.

3.1

3.2

MODERN PLAYGROUND

TIME LIMIT: 14 MINUTES

Kids are quite technologically savvy these days. In today's culture, with movies, video games, iPods, and computers, kids are becoming further and further removed from the playgrounds most of you probably remember from your youth. As kids get older and technology provides new avenues of playful diversion, jungle gyms and swings seem so antiquated—until now.

Your task is to create the ideal children's playground for today's tech-savvy youth. Draw out the entire playground and consider technology, weather, durability, safety, physical play attributes, longevity, and most of all, fun. You have no budgetary limitations; money is no object, so show these kids what playgrounds could be if you were Playground Design Chairman of the World.

THE MORAL

This is an exercise in subjective relevance. The degree to which the problem is solved is subjective and is left to the solver. The bare minimum is that something physical has to exist but what that structure becomes is entirely based on the perspective of the designer. How do you view technology as a play tool? Does it replace physical play, enhance it, or provide a distraction from it? The relevance of the solution isn't absolute; the minimum is so loosely defined that almost anything qualifies as a relevant solution.

This is a common scenario in ideation. You are often asked to solve problems that have subjective relevance scales. This is most often defined by the subjective eyes of a client who is acting as the gatekeeper between the idea and its introduction to the audience. The opinion of that gatekeeper plays a larger role in a solution's success than the actual solution. It is your responsibility as an idea generator to then define what constitutes relevancy. This may occur through a conversation or an experience, or it may require proof. Regardless, subjective relevancy turns novelty powerless unless it is distinct. Like a loosely defined problem, it may be virtually impossible to solve creatively if the success measure isn't outlined clearly.

SAY WHAT?

TIME LIMIT: 3 MINUTES

Have you ever sat at a table in a restaurant and watched from afar as a couple at another table conversed? It's natural to wonder what the topic of conversation is, especially if either party gets animated in any way. It's fun to imagine the conversation and even act out what each person is saying. So fun, in fact, you'll do it right now.

You'll need some form of video to watch for this exercise. It can be online, on TV, or on some other device. If no video is available, you'll need to watch at a distance two or more people having a conversation that you can't hear. If you're using a video, find one with a scene of two or more people talking and turn off the sound. This will work best if you find a scene that is unfamiliar to you. For the next three minutes, make up the dialogue that is occurring between the characters. Be the voice of each character you see, and invent a possible scenario on the spot. Do this without stopping or pausing, say it out loud, and just make it up as you go along.

THE MORAL

There's only one way the result of this exercise wasn't funny: And that is if it wasn't relevant to a scenario. You could have solved this problem by simply filling space with mindless dribble, but it's best if you wrapped the conversation around an event or relationship. There should have been some central theme you immediately found, and everything in that conversation had to do with that theme. If so, the entire conversation was relevant to this theme. If not, the result wasn't a relevant solution regardless of how novel the words may have been.

This is known as comparative relevance. The relevancy of the solution can only be compared to the event in which it is applied. Each sentence you injected was part of the overall relevancy of the solution compared to the sentence before and the situation created. This is where authenticity defines relevancy. If the response from one character isn't authentic to the situation, the whole solution falls apart.

An old advertising saying sums up the goal: "Don't worry about being different. Be authentic and different won't matter." As you generate ideas, remember that authenticity, another word for relevancy, must exist for novelty to matter.

3.4

PHOTO NEMESIS

TIME LIMIT: 12 MINUTES

Every superhero has a nemesis—that one villainous adversary that seems to give the hero the most trouble. The archenemy is the anti-hero, the yin to the hero's yang. It is possible that even you have a nemesis, someone in your life who seems to be your polar opposite and works to undermine you at every turn as you thwart your foe's dastardly advances and live to fight another day. Even inanimate objects can have a nemesis, that opposing force that could be defined as its seminal contrast. It's time to find these adversaries.

You'll need a smartphone with a camera or a digital camera for this exercise. Your task is to find and document an object and its nemesis photographically. It may help to find an object in your area first and then consider what its nemesis object would be. If your solution is available, shoot both subjects next to one another in one photo. If your solution is unavailable, find another object and start the process over until you can photograph your objects together.

THE MORAL

Did you stretch the truth in this exercise? It's a common response because it is the type of exercise that encourages rationalization. You can make any two objects philosophical opposites if you frame them the right way. The challenge is to find others who would qualify that reasoning as well.

In the ideas that you generate, it is common for you to want to "stretch the truth" to solve a problem, especially if you have a solution that you like already in mind. If it isn't fully relevant, you'll spin the reasoning to try to insert artificial relevance to bridge the gap. Watch out for this easy behavioral shift. Relevance should be predefined, not molded after the fact.

STICK!

TIME LIMIT: 8 MINUTES

Introducing "Stick!" Stick! is the hottest new toy on the market. Kids love Stick! They can't get enough Stick! Stick! sells millions of "units" every month. It's sweeping the nation—at least it will when you convince your audience that it is. Forget that it's really just a common stick that you would find at the base of any tree. You need to create headlines for the print ad that introduces the world to Stick!

Your task is to create as many headlines as you can for a print advertisement marketing Stick! You have to sell Stick! to kids everywhere, so consider the language you should use that would compel kids to read more about this amazing new toy.

THE MORAL

As you developed ideas for this exercise, did you self-critique your responses or did you record everything on paper regardless of how good or bad you thought your ideas were? Problems like this benefit from volume, but it's difficult not to judge solutions as they come to mind, filtering what you think is relevant and what you think sucks. The truth is you should have generated at least eight headlines in these eight minutes. If you didn't, there's a good chance you were self-critiquing, attempting to gauge the novelty and relevance of each solution as it was generated. Although this may lead to more formed solutions, the volume of novel alternatives will suffer.

Removing self-critique is one of the hardest steps in creative training. You've spent a lifetime training yourself to "think before you act." This is useful in staff meetings but not in creative exercises. During ideation, learning to turn off your judgmental inner voice will provide a greater quantity of responses that could offer nuggets of future solutions. This occurs only if you're willing to get them out of your head and onto paper.

3.5

PROGRESS EXERCISE

Enter your solutions into the Section 3 Progress Exercise guide from your dashboard at www.creativebootcamp.net to keep track of your creative progress.

RED

TIME LIMIT: 3 MINUTES

They say a rose by any other name is still a rose. I say there's a lot in a name. You'll find out exactly how much.

For your section progress exercise, you'll write down as many words as you can conjure that describe the color red. They can be alternate names for red or simply analogies for the color. Imagine that you have to convince someone to say the word "red" without saying it yourself. Write down as many words as you can in three minutes.

SECTION **3**

ROUNDUP

This week you discovered the varying degrees of relevance that exist within your ideas. You can't focus on novelty if relevance is missing from your ideas, so it is important to define what constitutes a solved problem before turning to novelty to up the creative quotient. Let's recap what you learned this week.

WHAT'S NEXT?: History plays a role in any solution you generate. You should consider the history of not only the solutions that have come before, but also the history of the problem. You may find that what you believe to be relevant actually falls short.

 MODERN PLAYGROUND: It's commonplace for clients to act as the gatekeeper for ideas. This subjective relevance can be frustrating if you don't take the time to define what a relevant solution is before you begin to solve a problem. Asking a simple question to establish baseline expectations can save you a world of hurt as you solve problems.

SAY WHAT?: Are the ideas you generate authentic? Authenticity defines relevance in most cases. If the ideas you generate aren't authentic to the situation, no manner of novelty will be able to generate a creative outcome.

PHOTO NEMESIS: Don't back your solutions into the problem. It is common to slightly mold and shape a problem to fit a predefined solution simply because you like the solution. Make sure the solution actually solves the problem.

STICK!: Self-critique will kill creative spirit. Creative coach and *Do-It-Yourself Lobotomy* author Tom Monahan separates ideators into two categories: shotgunners and riflemen. Shotgunners spray an idea with every possible idea or germ of an idea, whereas riflemen hold their ideas to themselves until they've formed a perfect, hole-free solution. Be a shotgunner. Having more to choose from can inform future solutions, but only if those possibilities are on the table.

Congratulations! You've passed the halfway point of the program. I'll ratchet up the difficulty a little to keep you challenged and in tip-top creative shape. In Section 4, you'll explore restriction and find out firsthand the effect escalating restriction has on ideation.

SECTION 3

THE CREATIVE BARBELL

As mentioned earlier, restrictions are necessary for creativity to be present. In fact, the more restrictions placed on a problem, the greater the opportunity for a creative solution. Restriction also plays a role in the idea of creative training. Think of it like physical training.

When you go to the gym, you lift weights to increase your strength. As you get stronger, you increase the amount of weight that you lift to challenge your strengthening muscles. It is the repetitive resistance that breaks down the muscle to give it a chance to rebuild stronger. Restrictions related to problem solving provide the resistance your creative mind needs to break down and rebuild stronger.

To solve problems with novelty and relevance, you should start with easier problems. As you solve them, you'll get stronger and can therefore "up the weight" or increase the restriction associated with the problems you solve. This makes them more difficult problems, which require more creative thinking to solve them. As a result, you reach new problem-solving strengths.

In this fourth week, the level of restrictions will be elevated in the exercises you are asked to perform. At the conclusion of the week, you will complete a section progress exercise that will help gauge your progress through the program. Be sure to enter your responses into your training program guide at www.creativebootcamp.net.

4.1

THE SQUIGGLE

TIME LIMIT: 4 MINUTES

The squiggle is the oldest and simplest of creativity exercises. The basic premise is to turn chaos into order—to see form in a formless shape. But I'll add a couple restrictions to ensure that you are being creative, not just artistic.

Using the hand you don't use to write with, create a random squiggle on a piece of paper. You'll turn this squiggle into something real. Avoid creating an abstract drawing, like simply filling in shapes or adding decorative features; that's doodling. The result needs to be something real. You can turn the page at whatever angle you'd like to move the squiggle so its orientation sparks an image. Now, using the hand you normally write with, place the pen or pencil on the paper, and without lifting the pen or pencil off the paper until you're done, finish the drawing.

THE MORAL

Did you draw something human, like a face? It is the most recognizable visual form in the world, and the one you see most in visual chaos. It's also the easiest to complete because it is still recognizable in abstract form. There is a balance to the human face that is immediately noticeable, which makes it the simplest solution. But is it the most creative?

When you generate ideas, do you execute the first idea that comes to mind, or do you keep going, generating other ideas to see if there's something better? When you are presented with difficult problems, is it easier to push for more solutions? Do you do the same thing when you're faced with problems that seem simple? Next time you're solving a simple problem, take a moment to set aside the first solution that you think of and generate a few more. The first solution may be the best solution, but you'll never know until you have something to compare it to.

TREEMANSION

TIME LIMIT: 13 MINUTES

The simple and undeniable truth is that treehouses are wasted on the young. Why should children have all the fun that accompanies their own private, lofted residence complete with plank staircases and rope swings? Adults deserve a perched escape just as much as they do. Heck, they can probably have the house you're in now if you can build the treemansion of your dreams, right? Let's find out.

Your task today is to plot, scheme, and design your ultimate dream treemansion. It can look like and have anything you desire; money is no object. You have been issued an unlimited grant from The Federal TreeHouse Administration's hedge fund, and you have your kid's college savings plan as collateral, so get crazy. You don't need to know how to build it or even if it is possible to build. You just have to imagine and document it. The only restriction is that it has to, of course, be in a tree.

THE MORAL

Most people would say that they can't draw. It's a skill they simply have never mastered. Most of the adult world would say this, anyway. There isn't a kid alive who would say he or she can't draw. Why? Because kids just draw, and that's the only prerequisite to meeting the criteria. But they also have no problem seeing what is in their head within the picture that they drew. When they draw a sky, a rainbow, and their family playing on a grassy hill, they don't see their drawing; instead, they see the actual scene. It's not a drawing; it's a photo. However, adults have that inner critic that says it's not a photo; it's a representation and one that doesn't quite meet the picture in their minds. This is one reason adults limit the ideas they share. They can't document them.

In the exercise, were there ideas that you had for your treemansion that you didn't include because you didn't know how to draw them? I'm betting there were. If you were thinking large enough, there should have been inclusions that you didn't know how to document, so you simply chose not to include them. Don't let an inability to execute potentially affect which ideas you share, because in time it will affect which ideas you generate. You must find a way to document the ideas you generate, whether that is visually, textually, or verbally. Don't let what your hands can't produce keep you from expressing what your mind can conjure.

4.3

THE WHATEVER MOUSETRAP

TIME LIMIT: 15 MINUTES

The first commercial patent for the common mousetrap was obtained in 1897 and was called "The Little Nipper." It looked an awful lot like the current mousetraps, snapping a steel wire down on the unsuspecting and unwanted rodentia while they snacked. Today, there is a never-ending battle for a more humane way to rid our homes of the furry infestation. Every manner of contraption has been created, but very few were constructed from random riffraff.

Your task is to devise and build a better mousetrap out of whatever is within your arm's reach at this very moment. Humane and kind or deadly and devious, it's your choice. But know this; the trap must functionally work. Happy hunting.

THE MORAL

How did you start this exercise? Did you start by gathering potential building materials, or did you draw out a few thoughts? Did you get a basic idea in your mind, like capture, and start building, or did you survey the landscape to see if an object sparked a solution? The creative process is different for everyone; individuals make their way to the finish line in their own unique way. Although the important aspect is arriving at a solution, it's helpful to prototype rapidly, leave room for failure, and improve in increments.

The first step you should have taken was to survey the landscape to see what you had to work with (I have this bowl, a pen, and some office supplies) and then start to experiment with possible solutions. The second step should have been to break the problem into pieces and solve the pieces ("I can use this bowl for the capture and the pen for the stilt to keep the bowl up"). In the third step, you should have improved on the idea with newfound materials ("The pen is too tall, so I'll use this extended paperclip instead").

If you didn't follow this process, does it mean that your mousetrap is a failure? Of course not; but these basic steps will lead to positive creative results.

4.4

EMOTIGRAPHS

TIME LIMIT: 12 MINUTES

A pictograph is a picture that represents a word. For example, if I showed you a picture of an arrow, that is a pictograph representing, well, an arrow. Although simple in concept, the application can become more difficult when you add a simple restriction: abstraction.

Your task today is to draw six pictographs for the six separate words that follow. The restriction is that you can use only four straight lines and one circle to create each pictograph. The circle cannot be broken into pieces, and the lines cannot be divided to make additional lines. The lines can vary in length, and the circle can be any size, but it cannot be reshaped.

Here are the six words:

Anger
Love
Danger
Scary
Cold
Playful

THE MORAL

There is no right or wrong answer to this exercise, but the exercise is a creative challenge. You have a problem to solve and a narrow set of restrictions to which to adhere. In fact, this is very much like the problems you solve on a regular basis. Right or wrong does not apply, just degrees of relevance and novelty.

If you showed your solutions to others, most likely some would be understood immediately and some would require explanation. I encourage you to show someone else your solutions and then re-solve the pictographs that need explanation. Try to create a solution that can be identified immediately. This is exactly how the creative process works.

When you solve problems, do you reevaluate the solutions that didn't quite work? Or, do you blame the person to whom you were communicating for "not getting it"? This is a common deflection technique creatives apply when their ideas aren't met with approval. It's others' fault for misunderstanding. Although this may be true, there is still a problem that hasn't been solved with the relevancy that is needed. In the end, relevancy must established before novelty, so continue to generate solutions until it does.

4.5

ALPHABET STORY

TIME LIMIT: 15 MINUTES

You walk to your desk and see a package sitting on your chair. It is wrapped in brown kraft paper and tied with twine. On the top is a sticker that reads, "Open in private." You look around quizzically and don't find anyone you would describe as suspicious, so you decide to act.

This is the start to a story. One that you'll finish out loud and with one caveat: Every sentence you speak must start with a consecutive letter of the alphabet. So your first sentence must start with the letter A, your second sentence must start with the letter B, and so on until you complete your story with the last sentence starting with the letter Z. Tell the story audibly and try not to stop and think; just go with whatever comes to mind to begin the sentence, working it into the story so it makes sense.

THE MORAL

If your story didn't make sense, you're not alone. The restrictions regarding the letters make it very difficult to complete in a way that sounds natural, but that is the point. Odds are you had no idea how the story was going to progress, let alone finish. It takes courage to start walking when you don't know the destination. This type of courage creates idea seeds.

Idea seeds are the beginnings of ideas. They are the start without the finish, the possible without the knowable. They are typically left unsaid until they've been formed. But idea seeds have value beyond what they will eventually become. They typically start with, "I don't know where this is going, but what if…" and manifest as partial ideas, a piece of something larger if at all. Most idea seeds fall on hard, unfertile ground, but a few land in the right place and someone else is able to take that seed and plant it. It sometimes takes the experience and perspective of another to move an idea from possible to plausible. It may only be a piece to you, but it sparks something else in another who elevates it to new heights. If you never offer it, it'll never have a chance to grow.

This is why the unknown is such a great place creatively. You don't have to have fully formed solutions to offer creativity to a problem. If you are willing to start walking without knowing where you're going, you may provide the perfect seed for someone else to plant and grow.

PROGRESS EXERCISE

Enter your solutions into the Section 4 Progress Exercise guide from your dashboard at www.creativebootcamp.net to keep track of your creative progress.

AROMAN
TIME LIMIT: 3 MINUTES

Most men's cologne is designed to do one thing: smell nice to women. Without cologne, men smell less appealing. This is not news. However, the problem with most men's cologne is that it is designed for the 2 percent of the time when women are within sniffing distance. The other 98 percent of the time men would simply rather smell something else, something manlier. That's where you come in.

You have three minutes to write down as many possible cologne scents that men would rather smell on themselves. Think of the smells men love, and you'll do great.

SECTION **4**

ROUNDUP

This week you explored how elevating restrictions can make problems more difficult as well as make solutions more creative. You experienced how restrictions can lead you to solve problems in certain ways, can encourage surrender, or deflect responsibility. Handled with boldness, however, restriction can provide the kindling for a creative fire. Let's recap what you learned this week.

THE SQUIGGLE: Simple problems typically elicit simple solutions. But just because a solution is simple doesn't mean it is ideal. You should challenge yourself to question every problem that arises to ensure that what seems easy is truly most effective.

 TREEMANSION: It is common to let executional deficiencies influence creative output. Don't let the skills you may lack interfere with the ideas you might generate. Limiting your creative scope in this way will ensure that your talent never exceeds your skill.

 THE WHATEVER MOUSETRAP: Simple process guidelines help to ensure effective ideation. Rapid prototyping, room for failure, and solution improvement are general steps that can be integrated into everyone's creative process.

EMOTIGRAPHS: Take ownership if solutions aren't communicated in the way you intended. It's easy to blame the audience for not understanding the novelty behind the idea, so don't let that deflection blind you to a possible relevancy issue. Be willing to resolve the problem when views differ.

ALPHABET STORY: Don't be afraid to go down the unlit path. Human beings fear the unknown, but creativity thrives on it. Be willing to take the risk and share idea seeds to see if others can apply their perspective and experience to the solution and grow it beyond your capabilities.

You are just one week away from completing the program. The last week deals with unexpected associations and how to combine unlike elements to find creative solutions. In Section 5, you'll be heading down the homestretch to Creative Boot Camp graduation.

NOVELTY'S PENTHOUSE

In 2008, Honda carved strategically placed grooves across a stretch of a Lancaster, California, highway. The grooves turned passing cars into musical instruments as their tires played the finale of the William Tell Overture as they drove over the grooves at 50 mph. This was an unexpected experience for unsuspecting drivers, and one that most found incredibly creative.

If novelty was an office building, unexpected would be the penthouse. If an idea sneaks up on the audience and presents an unforeseen solution, that solution has achieved nearly perfect novelty. The solution is so new that no one saw it coming. It still has to be relevant, of course, but surprise is the natural human reaction to new. It is rare to generate solutions to problems that are completely relevant and completely unexpected, but it should be the ultimate goal of every creative.

In this fifth and final week of the Creative Boot Camp training program, you'll have an opportunity to generate ideas that are relevant and unexpected. At the conclusion of the week, you'll be asked to take your final exam and receive your final progress score. The remainder of Creative Boot Camp will offer some short-term, midterm, and long-term creative maintenance suggestions to keep you on the path of creative growth. Good luck.

EVERYDAY ACTION FIGURE

TIME LIMIT: 15 MINUTES

Action figures are typically reserved for comic book heroes and movie characters. There aren't many everyday action figures. Plumbers, schoolteachers, accountants, and others rarely get to see themselves inside a blister pack and attached to a card. But what if the everyday person did have an action figure? What accessories would accompany the figure? What special actions would it perform? You'll find out right now.

Think of an authority figure in your life. It can be a teacher, a boss, a parent, anyone who is above you in some pecking order. Your task today is to create an action figure for that person. Draw out the figure and the special actions it would perform. Include any accessories that would come with it to make it authentic. If it talks or makes sounds, what does it say? Create the authority action figure you know and include a few surprises.

THE MORAL

As you thought through ideas for your action figure, was it difficult to get past the obvious? Certain accessories and action features needed to be included to identify your subject as that person. But some accessories and inclusions were more specific to a deeper knowledge you have of that person. Perhaps it was a buzzword the individual always says or a particular habit. If you knew the person only on a cursory level, you may not know what these accessories or features mean. But if others knew the person the way you do, these additions make this action figure even more lifelike.

You should practice this same attention to depth when you generate ideas for others. Some ideas solve problems on the surface but don't go much deeper. Other ideas solve the problem intimately. It requires getting to know the problem in the same way as getting to know the subject of your action figure led to a more creative feature inclusion. If you're not getting to know the problem you're solving on that in-depth level, your chances of generating unexpected solutions lessen.

5.2

THE MIDDLE

TIME LIMIT: 13 MINUTES

One of the reasons everyone loves stories is that there is an understandable structure in play. You can comprehend character and plot and movement. You understand story so well that you can predict the outcome of a scene or story before it occurs simply by picking up the cadence of the story. If the story is a mystery and an unsuspecting college freshman is in the story and is walking slowly toward the creaking door to find out if the ax murderer is in the room, the voice inside you is screaming "WHY WOULD YOU GO IN THERE?!" The flow of the story leads you to make the implications you need to decipher what comes next. But what happens when there is a break in that flow, and you're left with filling in the missing pieces? Let's find out.

Your task today is to write part of a story—not the beginning and not the end. You'll write the middle of the story. I'll give you the beginning and the end to a story, and you need to figure out how to bridge the two. You have only three sentences with which to do it. Here's the beginning and end of the story; you fill in the middle.

> A man woke up in the center median of a busy highway unable to remember how he got there. He was holding an authentic 18th century Spanish sword in one hand and an empty bottle of peppermint schnapps in the other.
>
>
> Dazed, he picked up the chicken, apologized to the young woman, and rode away.

THE MORAL

In the many years I've been using this exercise, I've never heard the same story. Even with the same beginning and the same end, filling in the gaps is always a surprise. In most cases, the participants either get an idea of where to go in the first scene or what they will produce as the scene before the last sentence. Rarely were they able to see the whole picture before they began writing. It was the act of starting that triggered the creative solution.

This is true in your creative work as well. Action is the silent third requirement of creativity along with purpose and restriction. Action is an enabler; it forces you to solve as you go or you stall. If you don't know the end, start anyway. If you can see the end but don't know the beginning, just start somewhere and work backwards. Force yourself to begin, and set an artificial deadline if you need to. Just go. Sometimes, the act will help spur the idea.

FOR SALE:
MY CUBICLE

TIME LIMIT: 11 MINUTES

The secret to writing a successful real estate listing is language. If the house is small, you call it quaint. If there's no backyard, you highlight the spacious rooms. If it's missing a wall, it has outdoor charm. Anything can be spun to accentuate the good while downplaying the bad. You'll take this to the next level by selling your work area—not literally, literarily.

Your task is to write a real estate listing for your work environment. If you have a cubicle all your own, sell the features. If you share an area, sell the part that is yours. Write a listing that would make anyone not familiar with your work area froth at the mouth to take a look.

THE MORAL

As you wrote your listing, did you choose to ignore the obvious flaws in your workspace or did you choose to spin those flaws as something favorable? For instance, if your cubicle is right next to the men's room, did you fail to mention that little tidbit or did you say something unexpected like, "close proximity to popular hangouts"? As silly as it may seem, these are similar problems that you solve in your creative work.

The nature of any problem is that there is some obstacle that needs to be overcome. Often, that obstacle is a negative feature, function, or perception. It's easy to solve positive problems, such as how to sell a great product or bring awareness to a wonderful cause. Negative problems, on the other hand, such as how to overcome an overpriced product or circumvent bad PR to an otherwise charitable cause, are problems that you might shy away from solving but are in need of creative attention. Don't run from difficult problems. Identify all of the hurdles that need to be overcome, and use your powers for good to solve them.

5.4

OBJECT/ACTION/EFFECT

TIME LIMIT: 15 MINUTES

If you took the cap off a marker and then put that marker in your shirt pocket, it wouldn't be long before an ink stain appeared on your shirt. If you were holding an egg and then threw it out a third-floor window, there would be breakfast on the street below. Place a water balloon on your office chair and then have a seat. You'll be telling people your apparent bladder control problem is a myth. If you take any object and apply an action to it, some sort of effect will result. Let's test that theory right now.

Use the camera on your phone or grab a digital camera. Your task is to take three photographs representing an object, action, and effect. Take a picture of an object first. Then take a picture representing some action applied to that object. Finally, take a photo representing the effect of that action. To use one of the preceding examples, you could take a picture of an egg for your first photo. The second photo might be a picture of an open window, or a photo of you winding up like a baseball pitcher, or a picture of you looking out the window. The last photo might be of a smashed egg on the ground, a fried egg, or a policeman issuing you a ticket. Find a way to tell an object/action/effect story in three photos.

THE MORAL

This exercise represents the very core of creative growth. The concept of creative degree is in play here. There are obvious, easy solutions to this exercise, and then there are an infinite amount of creative degrees that you can apply. Let's take the marker/shirt/ink stain example for instance. The simplest solution would be an open marker, a shirt pocket, and an ink stain. But there are so many other variations, and each depends on the solution that comes before. You could use the first two images, and the third could be a topless guy, a laundry bill, a box of detergent, the shirt in a wastebasket, head in hands, duct tape over the stain, a bottle of correction fluid, or a pair of scissors. The potential effects are many, and all you did was just change the last image. Change the action image to a pants pocket or behind the ear, and you open up a world of new, unexpected possibilities.

This is problem design at work. By redesigning the problem, you can find new avenues for creative problem solving. Here, simply changing the middle action step unveils a host of new possibilities. In a way, redesigning the action step is a lot like moving through stages of The Pickle. The design of the problem can greatly influence the potency of the solution.

5.5

DANGERBALL

TIME LIMIT: 12 MINUTES

Rules are in sports to create a fair and balanced structure in which to compete. Without rules, sports would be chaos and there would be little competition. However, there are times when the rules in a sport seem to limit action or exist for safety reasons. Remove those rules or alter their purpose and the sport becomes very different—some would say dangerous. This is exactly what you'll do today.

Your task is to change three rules in any sport to make that sport ridiculously dangerous. I'm talking life-threateningly absurd—the type of rule change that ensures multiple casualties. Start by choosing the sport. Then change the rules, add new rules, remove rules, or alter the playing environment, uniform, equipment, or surface to create Dangerball.

THE MORAL

Unexpected associations often provide fertile creative space. Combining baseball with land mines or tennis with shark tanks can yield startling results. This exercise is a form of the word-web brainstorming technique, a method to try to force unexpected associations in an effort to spark creative thought. The idea is that if you put two unrelated subjects together, the novelty of the pairing could inspire ideas.

The word-web technique starts with the major subject of the problem in the center. Let's use baseball for instance. You would encircle the word baseball by writing words that relate to the sport, like ball, glove, bat, base, infield, outfield, and home run. Then you would write a number of words around each of those words. For instance, surrounding the word "outfield," you could write grass, throw, player, fans, wall, run, and catch. Repeating the process for the word "grass," you could write land, grow, seed, cow, green, mow, and flower. And around the word "land," you might introduce the reader to the idea of a mine. That's where you find the connection of two unassociated ideas, a land mine and baseball. This technique may not produce the solution, but it forces you to think of novelty first and then back into relevance.

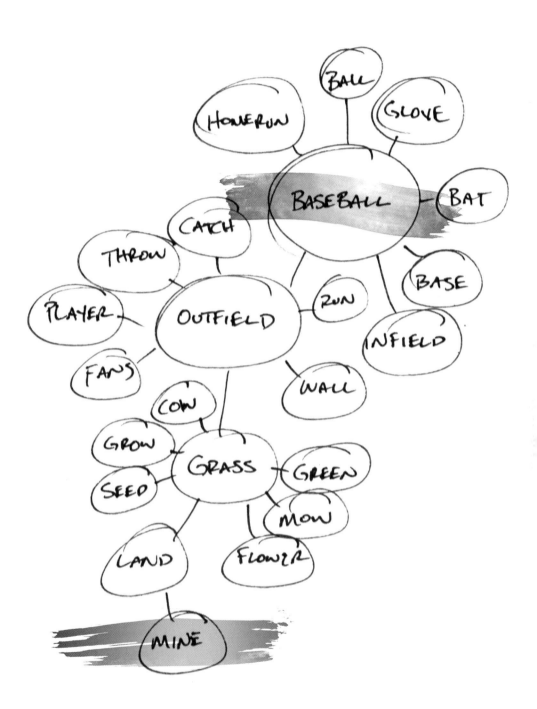

WORD WEB

SECTION **5**

ROUNDUP

This week you looked at the unexpected and how that
can trigger interest and novelty. Surprise is a powerful
influence, positively and negatively. If the ideas you
generate can create authentic, positive surprise, that is
the Holy Grail of creative solutions. Let's recap what you
learned this week.

EVERYDAY ACTION FIGURE: It takes effort to want to delve deep into a problem to produce solutions that are beyond the obvious. Getting to know the nuance of the problem will improve your chances at generating novel, relevant ideas.

 THE MIDDLE: If you are struggling to solve a problem, trust that you will find the solution in the journey and just go. Action is a facilitator. Use it to motivate ideation, even if that means leaving a part of the solution unsolved until later.

 FOR SALE: MY CUBICLE: It's tempting to walk away from a problem only partially solved, leaving the proverbial elephant in the room. Don't take the easy way out and choose to ignore obvious areas that need creative attention. Identify the problems that need solving, and solve all of them.

OBJECT/ACTION/EFFECT: Look for opportunities to alter the problem design in an effort to spark creative degree. You may be able to redesign even the simplest of problems to open a new world of possibilities.

 DANGERBALL: Unexpected associations are idea kindling. If there are times when ideas aren't flowing as freely as you'd like, look for opportunities to create associations that seem random as a facilitator to ideation.

You have only one more step to complete the Creative Boot Camp program: your final exam. The final exam is designed to test quantity and quality in the same way you have been tested in all of the progress exams. The format will be familiar and the subject playful. Complete your final exam, and then enter your responses into your training program guide at www.creativebootcamp.net. When you're done, be sure to read the next few chapters. They provide some resources and ideas for continuing your short-term, midterm, and long-term creative growth. Good luck.

FINAL EXAM

WILDWESTIOS

TIME LIMIT: 3 MINUTES

Remember the first time you found out there was a toy at the bottom of a cereal box? Odds are you mutilated that freshly opened box of cereal for the prize at the bottom. Nobody told you to just open the box from the bottom, oh no. You had to fumble through sugar-crystal-encrusted balls of crispy who-knows-what to get that bad dog. Nothing would stop you; you were a toy-finding machine. Would kids at other times in history have done the same? Let's find out what would have triggered their version of The Great Cereal Dig.

For your Final Exam, you'll write down as many cereal box toys as you can think of if boxes of breakfast cereal were around during the nostalgic era of the American wild, Wild West. From cowboys and Indians to horses and blacksmiths, the Wild West has a lot to offer breakfast cereal. Write down as many as you can in three minutes.

After writing down your solutions, don't forget to enter your answers into your dashboard at www.creativebootcamp.net to receive your final results.

THE AFTERMATH

SHORT-TERM MAINTENANCE

To maintain creative growth in the short term, you must be willing to insert conscious, purposeful change into your everyday. Creative training in the short term is very much like physical training in that there are passive and active steps you can take to maintain your endurance levels. When you run or walk, you can carry hand weights to strengthen or tone your arms and shoulders. The primary activity is the cardio, but the secondary, passive activity is the arm work. Short-term creative maintenance works similarly. Take the purposeful, active steps that require scheduling and time, and build in the passive, secondary steps that involve activity and opportunity, and you'll preserve the growth you experienced throughout the Creative Boot Camp training program.

The following pages detail active and passive steps you can take to maintain your creative growth. These steps are not intended to be exhaustive, nor are they designed to be an all-or-nothing approach. Make active what works for you and your process, but don't wait until the time is right or the stars are aligned. Procrastination leads to inactivity, so read through these tips and make the changes now.

CREATIVE BOOT CAMP BOOSTER PACKS

In the Creative Boot Camp training program, you survived 30 days of creativity exercises designed to present fun, engaging opportunities for creative problem solving. Through this practice, you developed skills that you use every day by solving problems with defined purpose and escalating restriction. Now that you've solved those 30 exercises, it would be far less fruitful to go back through the program and solve those problems again. The solutions you already generated would taint any future solutions. Wouldn't it be great if there were another set of 30 exercises you could complete that would challenge you in the same way? Well, I've provided just the thing: Creative Boot Camp Booster Packs.

On the Creative Boot Camp website, you'll find a series of available Booster Packs; each offers 30 creative exercises. The Booster Packs even come in different themes depending on your interest. There are Booster Packs for design, writing, and photography, as well as those same exercises divided into three Mixed Medium Booster Packs of escalating difficulty similar to what you experienced in Creative Boot Camp.

It takes passion to seek out problems to solve and then solve them creatively. If you're having trouble getting started, the Booster Packs provide problems that need solving; therefore, you can continue training yourself to be more creative. But these exercises and creative growth are not mutually exclusive. You can invent problems to solve by creating your own exercises or you can (gasp!) solve *real* problems. The problem being solved isn't the catalyst to creative growth any more than the barbell is the catalyst to physical growth. It is the action that defines the progress. If you need problems to solve to initiate that action, the Booster Packs are a great resource.

BOOKS

Just in the short time we've been together, I've established two very important qualities about you (I know, it's a gift): You are reading this book, so it's clear you know how to read, and you aren't opposed to books that focus on creativity and ideation. These two details are important because a cornucopia of literature is available on the topic of creativity and ideation, books that do the subject justice and are worth picking up and reading if you haven't done so already. The quest for knowledge should never end. You grow based on what you do with what you know. If you want to continue to grow creatively, here are a few suggestions that make great companions to the topics I've been discussing:

- *IdeaSpotting: How to Find Your Next Great Idea* **(HOW Books, 2006) by Sam Harrison.** Harrison takes you through a journey of recognition, teaching you to spot where the inspiration for great ideas lies and how to call out these ideas. He provides practical application to the habit of creativity and offers genuine, sound advice on creative growth.

- *The Accidental Creative: How to Be Brilliant at a Moment's Notice* **(Portfolio Hardcover, 2011) by Todd Henry.** Henry lays out why creativity is important and what is keeping you from being your most creative every day. He provides sound advice on process refinement and lifestyle change that will give you a solid foundation for generating ideas on demand.

- *inGenius: A Crash Course on Creativity* **(HarperOne, 2012) by Tina Seelig.** Seelig is a Stanford professor who spends a great deal of time teaching creativity to her students and business leaders alike. *inGenius* breaks down creativity into definable, actionable parts for the sole purpose of rebuilding it as a natural, everyday skill you can possess and wield.

- *Making Ideas Happen: Overcoming the Obstacles Between Vision and Reality* **(Portfolio Hardcover, 2010) by Scott Belsky.** Belsky takes a different angle on creativity: what happens after the idea. He defines how to see ideas through to fruition, providing the action to the ideation. The executional focus will help you take control of your creative growth and see the tangible results.

ROUTINEBUSTERS

Famed choreographer Twyla Tharp once said, "More often than not, I've found, a rut is the consequence of sticking to tried and tested methods that don't take into account how you or the world has changed." The problem is that you don't realize that your world has changed, and it changes every day. Despite this, you create routine in your life; your behavior becomes predictable. This in and of itself is not bad; routine is not an evil device. Routine enables your mind to focus on new problems while you perform familiar functions. But routine can inhibit your ability to see your everyday through the eyes of a child, with new perspective. And as you've learned, your everyday is a bastion for creative inspiration. To force yourself into seeing your everyday with this desired perspective, you must learn to break your routines.

However, routines have a natural cloaking device built in. It is difficult to recognize the very routines that you engage in every day because they've become second nature. When nutritionists want you to recognize what you are eating daily, it requires keeping a food journal to acknowledge the specificity of your food intake because you don't keep track of everything you eat. You remember the burrito but forget about the chips and Coke that accompanied it. To unveil routine from its innate camouflage, you first need to identify which behaviors in your life are routines.

You have daily, weekly, and monthly routines. Start with your daily routines. Do you wake up at the same time, perform the same morning rituals, patronize the same coffee shops, take the same routes to work, break at the same time, lunch in the same places with the same people, attend the same meetings in the same places, listen to the same radio stations, stop at the same watering holes or gyms and perform the same actions, eat or drink the same things, watch the same shows or listen to the same music, and go to bed at the same time? These are all routines. Identify them and then move on to identify your weekly and monthly routines.

Once you've identified them, make a conscious effort to change one each day, each week, and each month. On Monday, take a different way home. On Tuesday, go to lunch with someone new. On Wednesday, take a different class at the gym, and so on. The routine shakeup doesn't have to last. You can simply engage in that change for a day and then return to your regularly scheduled program, but do so purposefully and then move on to a different routine. The act of change has positive effects on your creative levels. You are training yourself to be more alert; therefore, you'll see opportunities you may have missed otherwise.

GET HANDY

Lego Serious Play is a successful group ideation and innovation method that uses Legos to facilitate problem solving. It is designed around two fundamental truths: Everyone can contribute to solving a problem if they share a common language, and the mind is more engaged in problem-solving activities when the hands are active. Most likely, you rarely associate creative problem solving with busy hands, but the two are uniquely linked. Simply put, you think better when your hands are active. For this reason, when I lead brainstorming sessions, I always have something on the table for participants to play with. From Legos to arts-and-crafts materials, having something available to keep participants' hands busy staves off unproductive distraction and enables their creative minds to focus on the problem at hand. It seems counterintuitive to provide what seems like a distraction in an attempt to deter distraction. But if you give your hands something to do while your mind is working, you're less likely to pour precious thought into something else.

As a passive step to short-term creative maintenance, fill your creative space with hands-on materials to play with and bring them to brainstorming sessions. I keep a one-gallon bag of markers, molding clay, pipe cleaners, rubber bands, paper clips, clothespins, and paper cups at my desk, so when I'm generating ideas for a project, there's always something for me to make or build. Sometimes, the results are sculptural, like the monsters you made in the training program. Sometimes, the results are just items bound together for no reason. Usually, the making or building has no purpose. It is just an act of creation that is meant to mirror the act of creation happening in my brain.

Doodling is another form of this hand/mind connection. The misconception about doodling is that it is mindless, but in fact, doodling is the result of a very active mind. You typically doodle when you are bored. But contrary to popular belief, your brain does not hibernate when you are bored. Actually, it is very active. Your mind is accustomed to processing information constantly, and when it is not stimulated, it searches for something to process. When you doodle, you give your brain something to process that allows you to simultaneously process other ideas because your hands are doing most of the heavy lifting. So don't consider doodling as an act of boredom; amplify your doodling. Doodle constantly. Leave pads of blank paper nearby, and doodle while you generate ideas. Keeping your hands busy frees the mind to find creative solutions to problems.

GET OUT

Illustrator Von Glitschka makes an analogy between new experiences and matchsticks. He says that every new experience you encounter is a matchstick that lights a fire in your creative being. He contends that you need to purposefully collect matchsticks by engaging in new experiences and then bring them back to your normal lives to burn when you need them.

Very few occurrences are more inspiring than new experiences. Your mind is most alert when you are engaged in a new experience because you have to process what is happening without a reference. It's those experiences that you often cite as most inspiring because those are the ones you burned brightest in your psyche. Therefore, it stands to reason that if you want to collect more of those matchsticks, you need to obtain more new experiences.

The mistake that is often made is believing that those experiences need to be substantial and take considerable time and effort. Not all new experiences require that level of investment. If you leave small spaces in your daily calendar, you can have a plethora of new experiences waiting for you when you need them.

Getting away from your desk and experiencing something new can be as simple as taking a short break or as involved as taking a long weekend. Keep a running New Experience journal either on your smartphone or in a notebook. Separate the listings into four categories: Break, Lunch, Day, and Weekend. Start by documenting what new experience you'd like to have if you had any of these four time increments available. For example, you might want to see a new exhibit at a local museum. If so, you can put that in the Lunch or Day category. Did a new coffee shop open near work? If so, throw that in your Break or Lunch category. Is a great workshop being offered at the Arts Center? Put it in your Day or Weekend category. Keep the list handy, because as you go about your everyday, you'll run across opportunities or items that you'll want to remember to put on your list. You may be out shopping and see something that interests you, so add it to one of the lists. You may pass an interesting architectural feature that you want to remember to photograph, so add it to your list. Dividing the list into those four time categories provides an instant catalog of choices when you *do* have some free time.

BECOME A GAMEMAKER

You explored the connective characteristics of creativity and play in an earlier chapter, and you learned about incorporating playful items like Legos and Play-Doh into your spaces. Play should be a natural part of your creative process and an integral part of your creative growth. But few know how to make play work. In Chapter 6, Kevin Carroll called it "strategic play," the act of forming play to mirror the problems you are trying to solve. But there is another way you can integrate play into your process: gamemaking.

Gamemaking in a purely play-oriented environment is the act of creating the environment, rules, and behaviors for a competition against people, time, or the actual player. In the context of a creative endeavor, gamemaking takes on a slightly more purposeful goal. Whether the goal is achievement or training, turning everyday tasks and problem-specific goals into games can begin to tie together the positive similarities between creativity and play.

As with creativity, a game needs a goal and restrictions. The goal defines the end of the game, and the restrictions define the rules and behaviors. Turning everyday tasks into a game means identifying and communicating those pieces.

For instance, let's say you were working on a headline for an ad in a shampoo campaign. Your idea is to play opposites, featuring what shouldn't be in shampoo to juxtapose the value in the client's product. To help generate quantity, you enlist three or four people in your group to help generate idea seeds for the headline. You could ask them to come up with a few headline ideas, but that may end quickly if they aren't writers or are unfamiliar with the product. Or, you could turn it into a game.

All you need is a goal and restriction. You could play a word game by dividing the group into pairs and giving everyone two minutes to write down as many oddball shampoo ingredients as they can with one restriction: The items must have the same tactile consistency as the shampoo. The goal is quantity, and the restrictions define the game environment and behavior. Because there is little consequence, the result may be ideas that are more creative than trying to extract fully formed solutions.

Once you've established some strategic games of your own, challenge others to do the same so you can play along as well. Engaging in play is just as vital to creative growth as becoming a playmaker.

MIDTERM MAINTENANCE

Have you ever returned from a conference or vacation and felt especially motivated to enact positive change in your life? You may have even collected a series of steps, actionable changes that you purposefully and thoughtfully made. These were most likely short-term steps to a long-term goal. Perhaps you wanted to improve in a certain area or pick up a new skill, so you took the immediate, actionable steps to reach that lofty goal, knowing you wouldn't reach it right away. You think about the long-term objective, and you create short-term actions to get there, but few ever think about the middle.

The middle consists of a combination of larger steps you can take as well as shorter goals you can achieve to help meet your long-term goals. These midterm directives require a bit of planning but usually don't require extensive life changes to achieve. If short-term maintenance involves steps to reach a goal, midterm maintenance involves strides that are both steps and goals.

In the next few pages, you'll learn a few midterm strides that you can use to help reach your long-term goals of maintaining positive creative growth. Some of these directives may be familiar, but even so, think of them as purposeful strides that move you forward in your journey toward creative maturity.

CLASSES

If you are a professional in your field of choice, the idea of going back to class may seem rudimentary. After all, you are a practitioner of your craft, an expert in some disciplines, and at the very least, as knowledgeable about the subject for which you produce as a classroom teacher may be. Although this may be true in execution, there is an infinite amount you can still learn conceptually.

I'm not advising that you take classes in your field of expertise at the local community college. Quite the contrary. I'm suggesting you take a class at your local community college in something in which you have little expertise. If you are a designer, take a class in story writing, photography, or even beginning guitar. If you're a writer, take a class in illustration or acting. The key is to find fringe classes that support your area of expertise by presenting similar processes in different mediums. As a designer, story writing teaches you how to find depth in the pieces of a problem, and beginning guitar teaches patience and progression. These are valuable skills that will benefit your core competencies and continue to push you toward creative development. And although there is value in the education, taking a fringe class produces creative side effects.

The very act of taking a class is a bold step, and there is creative value to taking bold steps. The more bold steps you take, the easier and more frequent the act becomes. If you are taking classes outside the realm of your expertise, you will likely be more attentive because the experience will be new. You will be practicing seeing through the eyes of a child. Bold steps bring confidence, and with confidence comes risk tolerance. But the effect of those steps are mitigated if you fail to follow through on them. For this reason, in-person classes are more effective for creative development. They contain a social accountability that online classes lack.

The odds are that you wouldn't take a class at a community college that didn't have a teacher who was grading your performance or classmates who were taking the class along with you. These two physical elements provide a level of social accountability that is sorely needed when you are taking a class for personal growth, not academic requirement. In fact, I suggest finding someone you know to take the class with you. This ensures that engagement stays higher than would naturally occur if you were left to your own devices.

Fringe classes take a few months to complete but are an invaluable commitment to creative growth, both intrinsically and extrinsically.

PASSION PROJECTS

Think of your ideal project. Form that project in your head. It's the one that would take advantage of everything you love about what you do and use the skills you have honed over the years while challenging you to learn not only something new but something you've always wanted to learn. Do you have it in your mind?

Now tell me, are you working on that project at your place of employment?

Probably not. The projects you work on at your job most likely touch on areas of your expertise, but few are used as training tools to learn something new. You're not typically paid to learn; you're typically paid to perform. For this reason, everyone, regardless of expertise, skill, or place in life, should undertake passion projects.

Passion projects are those that you usually take on the side; they are the nights-and-weekends projects you take on to either earn a little extra money or help someone out. They are called passion projects because you sacrifice *your* time to work on them, the time that is reserved for you. To do this, you must have a passion for the project.

Therefore, I'll suggest something shocking: *Don't accept money for them.*

When you accept money for a project, regardless of your interest in the project, the money will always be a motivating factor. Take the money out of the equation and you are doing the project for something else. Whether that something else is for you or another, the result is the same: You'll only take on the projects for which you find a personal attachment.

You can be passionate about the process, the subject, or the result, but you have to want to be involved for gains other than commerce. If your goal is to improve creatively, that can be your fundamental reason for taking on a passion project. You will then choose the projects that help you achieve those goals. You can form the restrictions in a more meaningful way and therefore affect the necessary creative input and output to a degree that paid jobs can't produce.

You can decide whether to take on long-term or short-term passion projects, but my suggestion is to take on more short-term rather than long-term projects. Short-term projects have shorter timelines; you can get in and out faster and therefore can find new projects with different opportunities. You can give only so much time to passion projects, so if the goal is creative growth, find opportunities to practice a particular characteristic or skill and then repeat the process using or building on what you learned or practiced.

TRAVEL CHALLENGES

Whether it is for work or pleasure, travel is an untapped opportunity for creative growth. When you need inspiration, you seek new experiences, and there is nothing more encompassing within new experiences than to be in an entirely new place. You are inherently surrounded by new and could be using all that new to awaken your creative senses and practice creative thought.

When you are traveling, develop creative challenges that encourage you to solve problems in places where you won't be tempted to produce known solutions. If you're away on business, take 15 minutes, walk around the hotel, and explore and document as many different typographic styles as you can find, or sit in the lobby and write down every sound that you hear. If you're away on vacation, make games out of sightseeing; for example, take perspective pictures of you or another holding something in the distance or only shoot pictures in a predefined time frame that are in the reflections of something else. These types of playful challenges will enable you to enjoy the travel experience while continuing to work out your creative muscles.

If you happen to travel with others regularly, encourage them to create travel challenges as well so that you can participate in activities of interpretation *and* creativity. This benefits the maker as well as the taker creatively.

IMPROV TRAINING

In Malcolm Gladwell's book, *Blink: The Power of Thinking Without Thinking* (Back Bay Books, 2005), Gladwell quotes improv theater founder Keith Johnstone speaking about what makes a good improv instructor:

> *"In life, most of us are highly skilled at suppressing action. All the improvisation teacher has to do is to reverse this skill and he creates very gifted improvisers. Bad improvisers block action, often with a high degree of skill. Good improvisers develop action."*

That last line has significance to creative development. Developing action is key to creative output. It helps move the idea from cerebral to physical. As you find an amplified confidence to shake the natural self-critique of ideation, you will undoubtedly improve your ability to generate ideas in greater quantity and quality.

As with many performance-based skills, improv is best taught by a skilled instructor who can identify the strengths and weaknesses of each student and adjust each person's education path accordingly. In a workshop setting, good improv instructors lead exercises and games in accepting environments that encourage participation and risk taking. When everyone around you is taking risks, it is easier for you to take them as well.

Improv training is an excellent way to challenge even the most outgoing of creative to grow. It is a bold step, it is social, and it celebrates risks and encourages failure. These are all beneficial exercises to creative growth. Learning to give up control is a humbling and powerful skill with clear ideation benefit.

ATTEND CONFERENCES AND TALKS

Although attending conferences and talks may seem like a no-brainer, it bears mentioning when advising on midterm creative maintenance actions. There is obvious educational benefit to attending conferences and talks, but it is the periphery benefits that I want to focus on here. Let's start with conferences.

Conferences are usually one-stop shops that consist of multiple topics within a certain discipline. Design conferences, for instance, offer multiple sessions on design-related topics, like photography, illustration, typography, or digital design. But ask any conference veterans to tell you what the most valuable part of the conference is and they will tell you it is not what is in the room but rather what is in the hall. Conferences are a unique opportunity for like-minded people from all over the country to come together to seek personal improvement. This network of similarly focused people is an invaluable resource in your personal growth. Sharing your goals and stories creates a bond of accomplishment and accountability that is often difficult to find in your "regular" lives. Think of it as an online auction site. If you have a rare baseball card to sell, you can put an ad in your local newspaper and you'll get the few people in that local area who may be interested in the card. But put that card up on an online auction site, and you instantly get a worldwide audience of people who have a sincere interest. Conferences bring together a broad spectrum of sincere interests. The networks you can create at conferences can help you get and stay on track creatively, provide consequence-free critique of a project, become ideation partners, and act as sounding walls for ideas.

Local talks are equally of value in the social sphere of creative growth. Every major metropolitan area has industry-based groups that offer speaker series or keynote talks. These, too, bring like-minded people together to learn and share but come with the added bonus of networking. The networks you create here can have an immediate effect on creative growth because you can get together for lunch and share ideas, call in networks for brainstorming sessions, or share regional problem-solving advice.

Apart from the obvious educational benefits of conferences and talks, the social profit is also of value if for nothing more than to create the next topic: creating a posse.

CREATE A POSSE

You know the term "posse" from Westerns, when the sheriff would round up a few like-minded people to help him capture the bad guy. Nowadays, the term posse is used for a similar group of people, but instead of gunning down fugitives from the law, these people can help you achieve your creative goals while you help them achieve theirs.

Everyone should have a group of people that they can rely on to provide insight, opinion, and, occasionally, accountability. If you don't have a creative posse, you need to assemble one. The perspectives and experiences of others are invaluable sources that can challenge you to understand and reach your goals.

Find five to seven people to meet regularly and discuss a common goal or topic. If you are a writer, you might meet once a month to discuss a project that you are all assigned to complete. If you are a designer, you might have an exercise that you all participate in over the month or have experiences that everyone can share. This type of group accountability ensures that you are working toward your larger creative goals.

The people in your posse should have diverse experience while still maintaining similar goals. Fill your posse with people who will challenge your position and have your best interest at heart. This type of selfless attention to the goal of creative growth will prove to be the most valuable step you can take.

LONG-TERM MAINTENANCE

The word January is derived from the ancient Roman mythological king Janus. In 153 BC, Janus was placed at the beginning of the Roman calendar. Janus had two faces, one to look back into the past and one to look forward into the future. Ancient Romans used Janus as inspiration to spend the beginning of the year asking forgiveness for past transgressions and exchanging gifts that symbolized hope for the year to come. This tradition has manifested itself in our present-day calendar as well. You know it as the tradition of New Year's resolutions.

Resolutions are long-term goals you set for yourself, changes you'd like to see in your life. They are easy to set and difficult to keep because you rarely set a plan in place to achieve these goals; you simply fill out the wish list and hope for the best. To make resolutions stick, you have to be willing to make significant change, not just willing to accept the benefit that change will produce. Long-term creative maintenance is like resolutions for the creative mind. They are goals that require an actionable plan, accountability, and faith that the journey is worth it.

In this last chapter, you'll explore a few long-term creative maintenance goals that you can set that will help you uphold a creative lifestyle. Unlike the short-term and midterm goals in previous chapters, long-term goals are more philosophical than actionable. The actionable steps will come in how you implement these suggestions.

MOVE THAT BODY

In his aptly titled book *Uncertainty* (Portfolio Hardcover, 2011), author Jonathan Fields details how exercise minimizes the effect anxiety has on the brain:

> *"Studies now prove that aerobic exercise both increases the size of the prefrontal cortex and facilitates interaction between it and the amygdala. This is vitally important to creators because the prefrontal cortex, as we discussed earlier, is the part of the brain that helps tamp down the amygdala's fear and anxiety signals.*
>
> *For artists, entrepreneurs, and any other driven creators, exercise is a powerful tool in the quest to help transform the persistent uncertainty, fear, and anxiety that accompanies the quest to create from a source of suffering into something less toxic, then potentially even into fuel."*

Exercise does not drive creativity directly, but everyone can agree that anxiety is not a positive creative trait. Therefore, if there is an activity or lifestyle change that can reduce anxiety, it stands to reason that it will have a positive effect on creativity. When you are fearful, you refrain from risk, and that alone will kill creativity. As Fields says, aerobic exercise helps turn fear into fuel.

Not only does exercise reduce fear, it builds confidence. As you set and reach goals, you will inherently feel more confident, and that confidence spills over into every other part of your life, ideation included.

Physical exercise is virtually identical in structure to creative exercise. Throughout this book, I've referenced physical activities as analogies to creative philosophies. Physical exercise requires that you set and reach goals, that you build strength over time, that you segregate muscles and work on them individually, that you apply rest, and that you change routines to keep the body guessing and the mind interested. Physical and creative exercise mirror one another in effect and time. And more important, each assists the other to reach goals. If you do not exercise regularly, I encourage you to start.

UNPLUG

Freedom is an app that does one thing and one thing well: It turns off the Internet on your computer. That sounds counterproductive because the Internet has become research Valhalla. But the Internet has also become distraction Valhalla, and distraction will keep you from achieving any and every goal you set (unless, of course, distraction *is* the goal; then all bets are off). You wouldn't think an app that turns off the Internet on your computer would be that popular, but over 300,000 people are using it. In fact, folks like Neil Gaiman, Guy Kawasaki, and Seth Godin are avid users. What do they have in common? They are all accomplished authors, creatives, and successful businessmen. Did the app make them successful? No, but the app is an analogy for something that did: They all recognized the benefit in living unplugged, even for a short period of time.

A common practice among successful creatives is a defined time and space for living unplugged and undistracted. Some have made conscious "no email" zones for the first hour of their work day, a time when they absolutely will not check or send emails. This enables them to get more pressing work done during that time. Others will sequester themselves in unplugged cabins or remote getaways to make sure they are spending solid time pursuing the creative work they want to pursue. Although you may not be able to control which hours of the day you check email or have the means to secure a remote cabin, you can set parameters in your life around your own forced unplugged times and places in an effort to reduce the blessed beckoning that the Internet emits in your life.

In his book *The Accidental Creative: How to Be Brilliant at a Moment's Notice* (Portfolio Hardcover, 2011), author Todd Henry calls this beckoning the "ping":

> "It's that little sensation that occasionally prompts me to check my e-mail or my social media accounts. It's the impulse to mindlessly surf news sites on the web when I should be doing something much more important.
>
> The 'ping' wants to be my master. It wants to own me. It wants me to serve it. And the 'ping' even has a ready-made life philosophy for me:
>
> Something 'out there' is more important that something 'right here.'"

Make a conscious decision to set aside some time or some place in your life when you choose to turn down the ping. Perhaps you can reserve an hour a day in the morning or at night when you can remove yourself from the distraction of the Internet and engage in some form of creative endeavor. Although the Internet has infiltrated your behavior and is a part of many things in your life, it's important to note that it can become habitual. Time is limited; there is only room in your life for so many habits. Make creativity one of them, and reduce the power of the distractions that keep you from creating it.

REORGANIZE LIFE PRIORITIES

A common New Year's resolution is life restructuring. Somewhere, through circumstances you probably can't remember, your life priorities have skewed. Where you once had time and space to create, you now have filled with all manner of responsibility, promise, and regret. Although you may not think so, you are in control of your own priorities. You can rearrange those priorities to steal away time and space to create if you are willing to sacrifice things that are less important to do so. This is the rub: You have to decide what's less important.

In an earlier chapter, I talked about input versus output. As creatives, you have to take in as much as you put out. Your fuel tank is a finite beast. In your life, are you leaving yourself time to do both, input and output? Both are required. You may be able to say that you have time and space to output but little to input. This is a common scenario that leaves you feeling shortchanged because you expend your creative energy without getting anything back. You may be able to say that you have plenty of time and space to fuel creatively but little to express any. This, too, will leave you unfulfilled because you have a well of ideas that never seem to be realized. You need time and space for both.

This is a difficult task because there is little in your life that you might consider frivolous. But with some active planning and an attentive perspective on the time you actually spend, it is possible in every situation to find time for creative input *and* creative output.

Start by thoughtfully examining your time. Write down exactly what you do all day, every day. This might be difficult but is a necessary step. How much time do you spend watching TV? Or driving? Or sleeping? If you are determined, there are blocks of time that you will discover you could trim. Could you watch two fewer TV shows? Could you find a way to reduce one day of driving? Could you go to bed and wake up a half hour earlier? These three steps alone would free up hours every day, time that you could apply to pursuing creative goals.

Sometimes, the time isn't that easy to find. But careful examination will provide opportunities to steal time that can add up to enough to input and output properly. Perhaps you can work an extra half hour every day and then spend Friday afternoons pursuing creative endeavors? Or you can take half-hour lunches and spend the other half inputting or outputting. Maybe make a rule at home that from 8:00-9:00 P.M. you get the office for your creative pursuits. Time is a bandit. Examine your life, and find the time necessary for creative inputs and outputs.

DO SOMETHING DIFFICULT

Have you ever worked on a lengthy project that you could dive into for months at a time, something significant that you could immerse yourself in and work all of the angles? These projects are challenging, but they are also rewarding because you know that not everyone could have done it. From writing a book to making a movie to building a website, time-consuming, complex projects have a unique fulfillment attached to them. They are also ideal for building creative strength.

Within complicated projects are a number of benefits to creative growth. First, perseverance is a key to seeing success. Creative growth takes time; you can't instantly achieve creative brilliance. Difficult projects typically extend over time, and they require focus over that time, which is often required for problem solving.

Second, difficult projects typically present continued, multiple problem-solving opportunities. Each opportunity presents a new set of purposes and restrictions that enable you to dramatically affect the outcome with every problem you solve.

Third, difficult problems aren't solved nearly as often as easy problems, so there is a greater chance at finding a novel solution.

This should be an attractive component creatively because there are fewer opportunities in your life to truly innovate than there are to solve problems ordinarily.

Doing something difficult doesn't exclusively mean taking on a tough project. Instead, it means finding something that will take time to overcome and then setting out to overcome it. You could take guitar lessons, learn another language, take up a cause, or rebuild a relationship. Doing something complex is a challenge to set big goals and reach them. This is a positive creative practice that will pay dividends across the board.

TAKE A CREATIVE VACATION

Yes, vacation. I know, now I'm talking your language. Few have a problem taking vacations but most don't have a creative purpose for vacation. Vacations rock because you leave responsibility behind, and entertainment is your only goal. This is a fine approach to vacation that will certainly help to recharge your batteries. But what if vacation was more than a retreat from responsibility but also a retreat from the problems you typically solve? I suggest you explore taking a creative vacation.

In 2010, I was asked to take a vacation to Kauai, Hawaii. To be honest, no one had to twist my arm. However, this vacation came with an additional opportunity. I was asked to create a murder mystery dinner at a 1930s sugar plantation for a group of vacationing salesmen and their spouses. Not only did I pack a suitcase with the normal Hawaiian vacation gear, but I also brought along my laptop and a host of murder mystery goodies to create the game.

Every day was a new adventure. Some days we spent driving the Kauai coastline, stopping at beaches and caves; other days we spent casing the plantation and hiring actors. It was a creative paradise, and a vacation I will never forget. I came back recharged and creatively fueled because I had taken an experience of complete novelty and used that experience to solve problems creatively.

Although the Hawaiian vacation may be an extreme example, there will be opportunities for you to turn a vacation into something greater. Plan a treasure hunt; write a short story; film a makeshift movie. Make your vacations a time to refresh and refuel physically and creatively. You will most certainly see significant creative growth from the experience.

FIND A MENTOR

It doesn't matter if you are 15, 35, or 85; having a mentor in your life is a good idea. A mentor is someone you can turn to for wisdom. Wisdom is a rare commodity; it is much different than knowledge. Knowledge is knowing the truth, but wisdom is applying it, and there are people in this world who have applied truth and can tell you all about it. Mentors don't have to be older, but they should be more experienced than you so you can take advantage of this wisdom. If you want to avoid the pitfalls that are inherent to every industry, find a mentor and tap that person's experience.

There are a few considerations to keep in mind when you're looking for a mentor. First, the mentor should work in your industry. Although your grandfather has worlds of wisdom, that wisdom may not be applicable to the struggles you face in your area of expertise if he hasn't experienced those same struggles. Second, remember that you are investing in your future, so even though that person may make considerably more money than you do, take your mentor to lunch and pick up the bill, or take the person to a game and buy the tickets. The experiences that a mentor can share are well worth the investment, and you'll be demonstrating this to that individual.

Third, don't call or email your mentor every week. Almost certainly, your mentor has others to mentor and is most likely still working in his or her craft, so be respectful of your mentor's time. Tap your mentor's wisdom when you need it most.

Finding a mentor may be difficult, but don't be afraid to ask when you've found someone you respect. And don't stop at just one. It's fantastic to find several people you can call on as mentors. The more counsel you can receive, the better you will be. You don't have to heed every piece of advice, but hearing from those who have traversed the same ground has obvious benefits.

Regardless of your place in life or your rung on the ladder, you, too, can become a mentor to someone, so do so. Mentorship is not age-specific; it is simply advising on the experiences you've had. If you've ever benefited from the advice of a mentor, be sure to pay that back by becoming a mentor to someone else. It is the great circle of creative life.

INDEX

courage, confidence, creativity, 91
Crackerjackimus progress exercise, 131
Creative Barbell, 162
Creative Boot Camp
    Booster Packs, 118, 195
    goal of, 116
    hand/mind connection, 198
    routinebusters, 197–198
creative degree, concept of, 184
creative growth
    core of, 184
    maintaining in short term, 194, 199
Creative Growth Score, establishing, 18
creative immersion, 3–5
Creative Katalyst, 82–83
creative limitations, fear of, 49–50
creative thinking, genesis of, 120
creative training, 85–88. See also training
    problem
    accountability partner, 118
    Artistic vs. Creative, 99–100
    Effort vs. Value, 102–103
    Input vs. Output, 99
    Inspiration vs. Motivation, 103
    Officer Booster Packs, 118, 195
    preparing for, 116–117
    Present vs. Aware, 100–101
    Pushed Forward vs. Pulled Back, 98
    Solution vs. Answer, 101–102
    tracking progress online, 118
creative vacations, taking, 217–218
creativity
    action requirement, 42–43
    commonalities with play, 83–85
    conditions required for, 32, 35
    defined, 148
    exercising, 116–117
    and improvisation, 88–92
    measuring, 17
    perception of, 20, 22–23
    and play, 80
    processes, 12
    relearning genius level, 23–24

    requirement of, 39
creativity is habit, 12
    Eat, Pray, Love, 22
    problem solving, 24–25
    quantity of ideas, 25–29
creativity measurement
    capacity, 108
    comparative scaling, 109–110
    sharing ideas, 108
creativity tests, 108–109
Crews, Terry, 98

D

Dangerball, 189
    moral, 186
    overview, 185
Dante's Inferno analogy, 58–59
dashboard website, 18–19, 191
"The Deep Dive" report, 7
    presenting result, 9, 11
    solving problems, 8–9
Design Disasters, 54
DiClemente, Carol, 97
difficult projects, attempting, 216–217
Disneyland, 40–41
dissected problems. See problem
    dissecting
divergent thinking, 86–87
The Divine Comedy, 58
"divine guidance," 103
Do-It-Yourself Labotomy, 161
domain of unknown, entering, 52
doodling, 199
Dr. Frankenstein, channeling, 135
dumb failure, 51
Duncker's Candle Problem, 34–35, 85–86.
    See also problems

E

Eat, Pray, Love, 22
Edison, Thomas, 5, 42
education and expectations, 28–29
Effort vs. Value, 102–103